Counseling the Alcoholic Group

COUNSELING THE ALCOHOLIC GROUP

by Joseph F. Perez, Ph.D.
Westfield State College

GARDNER PRESS, INC.
New York & London

The names and settings in this volume
have been altered
to protect identification of composite case material.

GARDNER PRESS, INC.
19 UNION SQUARE WEST
NEW YORK, NEW YORK 10003

ALL FOREIGN ORDERS EXCEPT CANADA AND SOUTH AMERICA TO:
AFTERHURST LIMITED
CHANCERY HOUSE
319 CITY ROAD
LONDON, N1, ENGLAND

Library of Congress Cataloging in Publication Data

Perez, Joseph Francis.
Counseling the alcoholic group.

Includes index.
1. Alcoholism counseling. 2. Group counseling.
I. Title.
HV5278.P47 1986 362.2'9286 86-440
ISBN 0-89876-131-X

PRINTED IN THE UNITED STATES OF AMERICA
DESIGNED BY SIDNEY SOLOMON

To my son Christopher,
master group counselor
and from whom I have learned so much
about alcoholism and the alcoholic.

Acknowledgments

I should like to thank two in-service professionals for their contributions to this book. Both Christopher Perez and Michael McCartney responded quickly and graciously to my requests. As the reader will see, their respective thoughts, together with those of the third professional who specifically asked not to be acknowledged, provide valuable alternative views of the alcoholic group, thereby enhancing the total work.

The person toward whom I am especially indebted is Marilyn MacKusick. She not only took time from her own busy schedule to type and proof read the manuscript but she also spent innumberable hours editing it.

Preface

Alcoholism counselors have discovered that group counseling is one of the most efficient modes of treatment for alcoholics—a discovery that has, in turn, increased the need for competent group counselors. *Counseling the alcoholic group* addresses this need by providing the information counselors must have if they are to function effectively as leaders for alcoholism groups.

To be effective the counselor must be very well versed in both the practical and theoretical aspects of:

1. The group process.
2. The dynamics and personal commonalities of the group members.
3. The functions of group leadership.
4. The techniques indigenous to facilitating the group.
5. Therapeutic activities for the group.

While there are many books that treat these items adequately, and some that do so exceedingly well, there are none that focus exclusively on the dynamics and problems peculiar to the alcoholic group. This book does precisely that.

Counseling the Alcoholic Group was designed both for paraprofessionals, or those without formal education or training, and for professionals—nurses, psychiatrists, social workers, psychologists, teachers. In sum, it is for all those who work with alcoholic groups.

The language, content, and style do not presume an in-depth grounding in psychological or counseling theory. The only presumption is that the reader wants to learn more about alcoholic-group counseling.

This book, then, is not only for the psychologically unsophisticated and the counseling novice but also for those who do not feel entirely comfortable with their groups despite their knowledge and experience.

Contents

Chapter 1

Definition, Value, and Rationales

A DEFINITION

THE CRITERIA for any good definition for counseling the alcoholic group are that it be both comprehensive and operational. For it to be both, the definition must take into account the counselor, the members of the group, and the nature of the process. In addition a good definition must answer three simple but critical questions: Who? What? Why?

Who?

A Counselor and a Number of Alcoholics Meet

Counselors must be trained and competent (Cohn, 1967). They are the leaders and are equipped to be the helpers, the facilitators, and the knowledgeable ones, and they are so seen by the members. The counselors are in a state of emotional congruence and are able to view each member of the group with unconditional positive regard (Rogers, 1961). Counselors are responsible "to" the members to lead, help, and facilitate group process. They are in no way responsible "for" the members, however, since members are, or must learn to become, responsible for themselves.

As will be seen in Chapter IV, successful group counselors are those who perceive their members optimistically. Such counselors have a need to help others, are willing to take risks in counseling, and are flexible.

Successful counselors are, moreover, people of conscience. Values and ethics are forefront concerns. They have a strong bent for introspection because they believe that a full appreciation of their own dynamics is a vital prerequisite for understanding and interpreting those of their clients.

The new group member is one who has stopped drinking. (Alcoholics who are still drinking are in a *toxic state*. In such a state, group counseling is an exercise in futility because the leader and the members are relating not to the person but to the alcohol.) Although they are unique, members are characterized by commonalities that set them apart from members of other groups. Chief among these is a distorted perception that leads to poor or nonexistent relationships.

In general new members are characterized by acute dependency, a sense of victimization and isolation. They also invariably have a demeaning self-view and are beset by an exquisite sensitivity to pain.

New members perceive threat everywhere and in everyone. For this reason they insulate themselves behind a thick wall of psychological defenses.

The most salient common denominator among the new members is probably their scrupulous consciences. This scrupulousness is usually newly found and a reaction to the virtual nonexistent conscience with which they functioned when they were drinking.

What?

Group Counseling With Alcoholics Is a Therapeutic, Interpersonal Process

Counselors can effect such a process when they are able to create a warm, nonjudgmental, sheltered climate where alcoholics can personally develop and promote in other members a sense of warmth, trust, mutuality, and acceptance.

Counselors understand that the group process occurs in five stages (see Chapter VI)—stages that blend and merge and through which each person passes in a haphazardly human way.

Stage one is characterized by member insecurity, hostile or childish testing of others, and fumbling methods of communication.

A feeling of place and position in the group, together with a sense of rapport with the group, signals the second stage. Communication is at three levels—verbal, emotional, and behavioral—but is seldom congruent.

The third stage is dominated by conflicts precipitated by the need to change perception of the self and others. There is a beginning awareness that the individual is responsible for his or her alcoholism. At this stage the members have progressed to the point where they feel that they can emotionally afford to air conflicts and direct energy toward finding out who they really are.

The fourth stage is distinguished by much hard and painful work. Thus the individual becomes involved in a broad spectrum of therapeutic activity—self-examination, self-disclosures, enhancing reactions to other members, and helping other members analyze, interpret, and resolve their problems.

The fifth stage is concerned with termination. Denial about self and alcohol has evaporated. Members realize that they do not need the group. They look and feel comfortable with themselves. Their newly found sense of emotional integration is such that they are willing to be themselves, and face being accepted or rejected by others.

Counselors facilitate this five-stage process when they are skilled in the techniques of group counseling (Chapter VI) and able to implement activities that are meaningful to alcoholics (Chapter VII).

Why?

So That the Alcoholic Can Achieve and/or Maintain Sobriety

This is the *raison d'être* for the alcoholic group. If the participants do not achieve both of these goals, personal growth is not possible.

In sum, the following is the definition that will be used for this book:

Group counseling is the meeting of counselor and alcoholics in a therapeutic interpersonal process so that the alcoholics can achieve and/or maintain sobriety.

THE VALUE OF GROUP COUNSELING

THE VALUE and benefits that group counseling can provide for the recovering alcoholic are:

1. The giving and taking of assistance.
2. Learning about oneself.
3. Catharsis (personal and vicarious).
4. Security.
5. Acceptance.
6. Enhancement of self-esteem.

The Giving and Taking of Assistance

Ohlsen (1970) observed that group counseling creates an opportunity for participants "to satisfy some of their strongest needs, especially in providing real assistance to peers while obtaining assistance from them" (p. 206). The giving and taking of assistance are in the best tradition of alcoholism counseling. It is the rationale upon which Alcoholics Anonymous was founded, and it is a major reason for AA's immense popularity and success.

In the alcoholic group, the counselor is not the only source of therapeutic help. Every member is a potential therapist. Every member is a helper. Alcoholics who are motivated to recover invariably experience and learn these facts. Typically they become devotees of the group by supporting and even promoting other groups.

Learning About Oneself

Another important benefit of group counseling is that it is a marvelous instrument to learn to deal responsibly with oneself (Trotzer, 1972). Alcoholics learn quickly that the leader as well as other group members are rich sources of knowledge. They learn that the emotional climate of the group is not only receptive but encourages exploration of their own and their peers' problems. In this climate they realize that their problems are not all that unique or peculiar and that their drinking problems are not a function of cosmic forces but were created by themselves. They learn that they are victims only if they choose to be.

Catharsis—Personal and Vicarious

Catharsis is the free expression of pent-up emotions by a group member. Such expression should be seen for what it is—a compliment to the leader and to the group because the member feels safe enough and is trusting enough to vent innermost feelings generated by repressions and fears.

Unfortunately, some group leaders view catharsis as a goal, and when it is reached feel that participants who have ventilated their feelings with this level of trust are ready to terminate participation in the group. Nothing could be further from the truth. Just as important as the cathartic experience is the reintegration of feeling by the individual, and this warrants at least several more meetings.

But Catharsis is valuable not only for the particular individual. As Hansen, et al. (1976) have observed: "Catharsis is one of the primary factors in developing groups' cohesion" (p. 262).

In alcoholism counseling personal catharsis can be, and often is, complemented by a *vicarious catharsis*. Members may empathize with the ventilating member because the hell that the ventilator expresses is one members have visited—or feared to. Although vicarious catharsis has value, it is not a substitute for the real thing. It is "spectator therapy" (Dinkmeyer & Muro, 1971) and group counseling must provide more than a mere show to be therapeutic.

Security

There are a number of reasons that the alcoholic group provides its members with a feeling of security.

1. The group members come into contact in a structured climate, one of "controlled intimacy." This facilitates and promotes relationships (Mahler, 1969).

2. The fact that there is a group ensures that no participant feels as if he or she is the focal point of attention.

3. Members derive a sense of power from the group. The group promotes the idea that they can lick their drinking problems.

4. Participants quickly find that the interactions of members are predictable. An alcoholic learns early when and how a given member is going to react, that phoniness is not brooked and that no one can be or is conned for long.

It is precisely for the foregoing reasons that participants "find it easier to discuss difficult subjects in group counseling" than in individual counseling (Ohlsen, 1970, p. 5.).

Acceptance and Cohesion

Acceptance is a basic human need (Maslow, 1970). Without it little is possible, much is difficult. As it is with the individual, so it is with the group. Hansen et al. (1976) point out that acceptance "is at the core of a successful group; without it there really is no group" (p. 259).

A sense of acceptance by the individual alcoholic can only promote group cohesion. It is cohesion that facilitates self-disclosure in the group (Stokes, 1983). It is cohesion that "enables parties to work on issues they could not realy grapple with in individual therapy" (Guttmacher & Birk, 1971, p. 553). The feeling of cohesion does not necessarily mean that all the members of the alcoholic group are good and fast friends (although friendships do develop). It does mean that all the members cognitively understand and emotionally appreciate that the presence or absence of each member alters the personality of the group. In short a sense of cohesion means that all the participants understand that their place in the group is secure until they are ready to terminate.

Finally, it is this feeling of acceptance by alcoholic participants that provides them with the emotional wherewithal to confront their fears and anxieties and to help other group members do the same. Acceptance and cohesion are indispensable prerequisites to group progress.

Enhancement of Self-esteem

The foregoing five benefits for the participant alcoholic inevitably lead to this last one. Group participants cannot help but be enhanced in their self-esteem.

According to Rogers (1961), positive self-regard is the need that transcends all needs. Thus in group counseling when alcoholics come to feel that they receive unconditional positive regard, the emotional climate is structured for them to begin to view themselves in this manner.

The need to increase self-esteem is especially important for alcoholics as studies show that they have lower self-esteem than nonalcoholics (Gross & Adler, 1970). Indeed the statistical evidence is strong that alcoholics just do not like themselves. What is especially ironic is that drink can only depress one's self-esteem, it cannot raise it (Konovsky & Wilsnack, 1982); group counseling does that.

RATIONALES FOR GROUP THERAPY

THERE ARE a variety of rationales for counseling a group. The effectiveness of a particular rationale will depend upon how well or how poorly it appeals to the counselor; that is, how it jibes with the counselor's background, training, and personality. The following brief explanations of the better known rationales are provided both to acquaint readers with their essentials and to show how widely different the approaches to counseling the alcoholic group can be. (A "Selected Readings" for each rationale considered are provided at the end of the chapter.)

The Psychoanalytic Group

Although still widely used, the Freudian approach to group counseling has never been a popular method with alcoholics. The complex, intellectualized rationale of psychoanalysis, together with the lengthy time necessary for treatment, has alienated rather than attracted most alcoholics. However, a description of the rationale is included here because much of its language, and many of its ideas and methods, have been adopted or adapted by other rationales. This is probably so because psychoanalysis was the first form of counseling.

In the psychoanalytic group, control lies with the leader. The leader directs, stimulates, and interprets group members' statements and behaviors. The focal point of the leader's concern is the *unconscious* of each of the members. Much time and energy are spent trying to fathom the "why" of the members' drinking. The view here is that there are root causes for an individual's drinking and the task of the leader is to get the individual to explore and uncover those causes. The problem is compounded by the fact that alcoholics resist acknowledging the real "whys" of their drinking.

Alcoholics are viewed as conflicted and neurotic. At the core of their neurosis is an *ego* so weak and inept that it cannot effectively mediate between *superego* (conscience) and *id* (the primitive, amoral, pleasure-seeking aspect of personality).

The analytic leader understands that the weakness and ineptness of the alcoholic ego result in a distorted *perception* and ineffective *defenses* that are the result of traumas experienced during the infant and childhood years. These traumas were *repressed* (buried and forgotten in the unconscious). The psychoanalytic view is that these repressions must be brought to light if the alcoholic is ever to stop drinking. To accomplish this the leader encourages each member to *free associate,* that is, to report memories, thoughts, and ideas as they come to mind whether or not they have any meaning to the alcoholic. The free association technique was adapted by Wolf and Schwartz into what they call the "go-around technique." Each person in the group is asked to go around the group and report first thoughts about each group member. According to these psychoanalysts, this facilitates rapport among group members and helps each person to understand better how he or she is perceived by other group members.

Resistance blocks progress. This is defined as "everything that prevents the patient from producing material from the unconscious" (Fenichel, 1945). Resistance is founded upon a fear of change and is manifested by alcoholic's argumentativeness, refusal to participate in group exercises, late arrivals, and protracted silence. Many individuals show resistance by hiding behind the analyses of others in the group. Such individuals often develop a talent for redirecting attention to those members who seem to be analyzing them.

Critical in group analysis is the identification and resolution of the *transference.* When in transference, the alcoholic perceives the group leader or other group members as the parental and/or sibling surrogates who effected or contributed to the alcoholic's repressions. The counseling group is an ideal setting for this because it provides the familial actors necessary to facilitate the transference process. In positive transference the alcoholic attempts to attach the feelings of love and warmth that were rejected by a parent or sibling to the therapist or other group members. Conversely in negative transference the alcoholic seeks to ventilate the hostility engendered by a demeaning parent onto the therapist or another member.

Transference by an alcoholic invariably precipitates feelings of *countertransference.* These stem from the group leader's unresolved neurotic conflicts, attitudes, and feelings. To react to the group with perfect objectivity is, of course, impossible. Therapists are human and necessarily will have reactive feelings to the members' negative and positive transferences. Even if the group leader were able to remain totally neutral, it would be inappropriate, because every group member wants the leader to become involved in the group, to express humanness. Complete neutrality by a leader would only effect more acute resistance, hostility, and alienation on the part of alcoholic members.

A prime techinque of the analytic group is *interpretation,* meaning that the leader explains the reasons behind the alcoholic member's actions and feelings. Simply stated, there is no psychoanalysis without interpretation. The leader recognizes when the emotional climate is appropriate for interpretation. A cardinal rule for interpretation is that the leader not only must know the client's history and dynamics, but must have a solid relationship with the group member.

Working through is the process by which transference, countertransference, free association, resistance, and leader interpretation become positively synthesized and lead to resolution of the group neuroses. Working through may begin as early as the first session. The process is structured to begin when the leader creates an atmosphere in which all the alcoholics feel free to express the feelings, attitudes, and fantasies that they have consciously or unconsciously kept hidden. The members come to understand their meanings with leader guidance. This understanding leads to an appreciation of the feelings that complement the problems expressed. This is called *uncovering.* The process of uncovering leads to the transference and the expression of the repression toward the leader and/or other group members. With expression and subsequent exploration under the leader's guidance, group members begin to connect their former repressions with their present lives and future expectations.

The Encounter Group

The major proponent of the encounter model is Carl Rogers. This method, popular since the late sixties, has generally found much favor with alcoholics becauses of its humanistic orientation.

Each group *client* is viewed by the leader as a peer who is in a state of *incongruence;* that is, the alcoholic cannot cope with drink. The leader believes firmly that all members of the group have the emotional resources to heal themselves. Unlike the analytic group leader, the encounter leader is a *helper,* not a healer.

All members of the group are perceived with *unconditional positive regard.* There are no moralizing, judgmental attitudes about client talk or behavior. There is only full acceptance of clients. The conviction here is that this full acceptance of the clients by the leader creates a healthier self-acceptance in the clients themselves.

A key element of the encounter leader's rationale is that the move to *congruence* from incongruence by members will be facilitated if the leader communicates *empathy.* Empathy is the ability to perceive the world through the eyes of the clients. Alcoholics live in a very lonely world. This "aloneness" greatly contributes to their disease. The leader who is able to communicate empathy enters the alcoholic's world and helps to dispel the alcoholic's aloneness.

Alcoholism counselors who are themselves recovering alcoholics generally find that they are able to communicate empathy without much difficulty because clients, both in the group and in private sessions, feel a mutuality and kinship in the alcoholic experience. Once leaders have entered the different, private worlds of the group, they find that they are able to promote security, a sense of "belongingness" and of self-esteem in the individuals and in the group as a whole.

Rogers does not believe that goals are an important issue in group counseling because each group has its own *actualizing tendency,* that is, each group will move toward health in its own way given the perception and rationale of the encounter group leader. A key factor in this rationale is the creation of a proper *psychological climate.* Such a climate is the one in which alcoholics need not be defensive but feel free to examine their lives and self-disclose their anger, fear, and suspicions.

Critical ingredients of the encounter rationale are *feedback* and *communication.* Alcoholism promotes furtiveness and distancing. Alcoholics too often have lost their ability to relate, interact, and communicate. This mode of group counseling focuses on the importance of recovering lost or never acquired communication skills. This is accomplished via feedback that usually comes in the form of *confrontation,* still the best technique with the alcoholic client. In the encounter group, confrontation occurs to demonstrate interest and concern for the other person. In every encounter confrontation by the leader, the distinction is carefully drawn between individual and act. The drinking is bad, not the alcoholic. Members of the group who confront their peers acquire this knack quickly.

The Gestalt Group

Fritz Perls was the founder of Gestalt counseling. Although he set forth his ideas in the early fifties, the Gestalt method did not become known until the late sixties when it was integrated into the human potential movement.

Many of the principles and activities of the Gestalt rationale have found favor with alcoholism groups. As a philosophy for group counseling, it jibes in considerable measure with AA's traditional approach to the alcoholic's therapeutic needs. For example, the Gestaltist believes that a principal reason for the individual's problems in coping with life is that he or she has not learned to accept and live each moment, each day, as it comes.

Goals are of vital importance in the Gestalt group. The principal one is to get the group members to mature, to take responsibility for their behavior. To do this they must learn to live in a *continuum of awareness.* They must learn to own their feelings and to be fully cognizant of their statements (idle talk is considered childish and always inappropriate). Most important in the continuum of awareness is a constant, exquisite sensitivity to body. Verbal inconsistencies with body are seen as attempts to shirk responsibility for one's feelings. Such inconsistencies are pointed out. "You say you are happy, but your look is an angry one." Healthfulness, then, lies in *wholeness,* in the integration of mind and body. If alcoholics are ever to acquire effective interpersonal skills, they must first learn to accept responsibility for their behavior. This, the Gestaltist believes, starts with the acceptance and integration of their own bodies. Once the alcoholics have done that, they can achieve the other important Gestaltist goal, to learn to live with anxiety, to learn that anxiety is part of the life experience. The leader helps by encouraging them to take risks and to confront both themselves and others.

The leader in Gestalt therapy is also the director of the therapy. Interaction is more often with the therapist than among or between group members. *The hot seat* concept illustrates this. Members are told that those who want to work rather than "screw around" (use of earthy language is encouraged) should take turns sitting in it. The leader interacts directly and aggressively with the alcoholics, one at a time. In this way each member gets individual attention, and is able to self-disclose to other members as well as to the leader. The other members in turn are able to learn about themselves vicariously.

A Gestalt therapist does not interpret a member's behavior. The focus rather is on the now and how. For example, a member might say, "Now I feel like I want a drink." To deal with the how of this feeling, the therapist might ask, "What specific feeling do you have as you tell me this?" If the member answers with anger or sadness, the leader encourages further perseverence. The rationale for this is that the more time alcoholics spend facing their neurotic, destructive feelings, the sooner they will be rid of them.

Body language is a constant focus of the leader. Thus the leader will ask the alcoholic who has been crossing and recrossing his or her legs for some minutes, "What are your legs saying to you?" By asking the question in this way, the leader does not interpret. Gestaltists believe that it is more important to keep all the group members cognitively and emotionally aware that mind and body are related, that what is going on in the mind is being manifested elsewhere.

A major concern of the Gestalt group is to understand and reconcile the *top-dog/underdog introjections*. These are attitudes and values that alcoholics swallowed growing up, the values that they took in whole. One of the reasons they need counseling is that they did not differentiate between parental or societal values and their own needs because to do so might have raised anxieties. In short, they never integrated the introjections into their personality.

Top-dog introjections are founded upon a puritanical-like righteousness. At best they are the shoulds upon which most people operate and are roughly equivalent to conscience. An excessive number of unintegrated top-dog introjections result in such qualities as manipulation, suspiciousness, and authoritarianism—all common characteristics of the alcoholic.

Top dog and its antithesis underdog constantly battle for control of the person. When underdog is able to control top dog, the alcoholic is in an apologetic mood, is unnecessarily defensive, communicates feelings of persecution, and procrastinates. The alcoholic's underdog is best seen in stubborn and passive-aggressive behavior, in goals not achieved and promises (to self and others) not kept. When the conflict between the two becomes acute, the alcoholic drinks to escape the recrimination (guilt) that top dog inspires.

There are three techniques that are used to deal with unintegrated introjections. Members are asked to differentiate between the "I" and "You." They are asked to make up sentences beginning with "I." The Gestaltist believes that such sentences build up the sense of self. Secondly, they are encouraged to self-disclose and thereby share the specific nature of their private agonies and temptations. It is by sharing their feelings with others that health is promoted and anxiety abated. Last, they are asked to put the conflict between their top dog and underdog in dialog form.

Dialog using the *empty chair* is an important Gestalt technique. Alcoholics invariably labor harshly under an excessively strict top dog. In the Gestalt group, they would at some point put their respective top dogs into the empty chair and talk to them with the rest of their persons. This technique enables alcoholics to get more accurate and realistic perspectives on the position top dog has and should have with respect to their total persons. By putting top dog or any other aspect of themselves into the chair, alcoholics are able to experience being that aspect and not just talking about it. It is through such dialogs that the feelings and various aspects of those feelings (top dog, underdog) become more fully integrated into the total person.

Critical in the Gestalt process is that each alcoholic learn to relate both within and without the group via *I and Thou*. The idea here is that self-identity is enhanced when people share feelings and self-disclose their personal anxieties. This process of sharing has an especially important benefit for alcoholics as it invariably promotes trust, a commodity that most alcoholics are short on. Gestaltists believe that trust develops naturally and inevitably when people learn to perceive others wholely, as important and as unique. To promote trust individuals are instructed to "talk to" and not "talk at" each other and to address others by name. Leaders point out that when the verbal content and tones of group members do not jibe (i.e., angry words spoken gently), they are avoiding communication with other members because they are not trusting and are not promoting a sense of trust in others. The "I and Thou" method of relating helps to strip away feelings of aloneness and distance. Finally, Gestaltists view the "I and Thou" approach to interpersonal relationships as critical if the individual is to achieve *authenticity*. Being authentic means being and acting as the whole self. It means being emotionally, physically, and mentally integrated. Authenticity can be achieved only if alcoholics learn to be keenly sensitive to their own bodies, feelings, and the effect of their talk upon other members of the group.

The Transactional Analysis Group

Eric Berne is the person responsible for the development of the rationale of transactional analysis TA). His most noble contribution to counseling theory was the discovery that each person operates with three separate but related ego states: *child, parent,* and *adult.* Each of these egos is characterized by its own interpersonal ways, dispositions, and talk. All people operate with one of these at any given time. The egos seek *strokes,* that is, reward and recognition that the person not only exists but is important.

People transact for their strokes in a variety of ways. They can *withdraw* and obtain their strokes with fantasy, a favorite alcoholic method.

They engage in *rituals.* These involve no more than an exchange of the predictable proprieties, that is, the passing morning exchange. "Hi, how are ya?" "Good, and you?" Both people in such an exchange can receive their strokes without effort or personal involvement.

Pastimes are also a common method and, like the rituals, demand little or no sharing or involvement. Discussions that involve weather, stamp collecting, sports heroes' achievements, or TV soap operas are examples. The pastime, like the ritual, is a favorite alcoholic method of transaction, especially when the person is drinking.

Activity involves seeking strokes through one's job or one's daily routine. To the transactional analyst, the hardworking alcoholic is a person with an insatiable need for strokes or one who has no other way to acquire them.

The most common way to set strokes is to play *games*. Game playing involves being able to give and receive mixed messages effectively. There is a payoff for every game played and the particular payoff characterizes the individual's racket (i.e., interpersonal style). Thus, for example, the alcoholic male who is in a constant, latent state of anger at the neighborhood bar plays the bully when it suits him as he knows who is vulnerable and when. Often this person has a drinking buddy who plays the submissive sidekick. Both get payoffs from their games. For the first, the payoff is a feeling of power, and for the second, "nobody loves me." The payoffs provide a motive for each to continue drinking.

According to Berne (1966), people decide early in life what their *life position* will be. These are four possible positions.

1. *I'm O.K.—You're O.K.* The person who holds to that position is one who feels secure and accepted, and functions with a good self-esteem. Such a person enhances others. The goal of TA is to get all the members of the alcoholic group to achieve this position.

2. *I'm O.K.—You're not O.K.* This is a position held by the interpersonally condescending and the suspicious. It is the position often held by the drinking alcoholic. Frequently, it is the perspective of the abused adult children of alcoholics who learned from their abuse that they were not O.K.

3. *I'm not O.K.—You're O.K.* Many, if not most, alcoholics, hold to this idea, if not manifestly, then certainly latently. Most often they developed it during childhood when they learned in a myriad of ways and for an infinite number of reasons that they were not O.K.

4. *I'm not O.K.—You're not O.K.* This is the belief shared by those who feel hapless, helpless, and hopeless. Unfortunately it is what alcoholics think in their sober moments and it is the position that leads them back to drink.

Once the life position is taken, the individual develops a *life script*, that is, a plan for life. It is with this script that the person seeks to obtain justification for the life position held and the strokes necessary to get through life. Alcoholics are so precisely because their life script does not enhance them.

There are three general goals for participants in the TA group: (1) to decontaminate the ego state, that is, to help each member rectify distorted feelings and perceptions: (2) to encourage participants to use the three ego states appropriately and flexibly; (3) to help members rewrite their respective life scripts so that they can engage in productive lives.

The Eclectic Group

Eclecticism is the final rationale that will be considered and it is the one that serves this book. This rationale borrows ideas from the preceding rationales and creates new methods that can facilitate and enhance the counseling of the alcoholic group.

Eclectic group leaders of alcoholics are not bound to any particular rationale. Nevertheless they have an in-depth understanding of those aspects of group counseling that are crucial to helping the group function effectively.

1. The dynamics of the alcoholic group.
2. The qualities and functions of the group counselor.
3. The theoretical bases of the group.
4. The stages of group process.
5. The techniques of counseling a group.
6. The activities that facilitate and accelerate progress with the alcoholic group.

These aspects will be treated in the following chapters.

SUMMARY

THE OPERATIONAL definition for this book is: Group counseling is the meeting of counselor and alcoholics in a therapeutic interpersonal process so that the alcoholics can achieve and/or maintain sobriety.

The alcoholic derives value and benefits from group counseling. These include the giving and taking of assistance, learning about oneself, personal and vicarious catharsis, security, acceptance, and the enhancement of self-esteem.

Among better known forms of group counseling are psychoanalysis, encounter, Gestalt, transactional analysis, and eclecticism, (the rationale used in this book).

REFERENCES

Berne, E. *Principles of Group Treatment.* New York: Oxford University Press, 1966.

Cohn, B. (ed.) Guidelines for future research on group counseling in the public school setting. Washington, D.C.: American Personnel and Guidance Association, 1967.

Connor, R. G. The self-concepts of alcoholics. In D. J., Pittman and C. R. Snyder (eds). *Society, Culture and Drinking Patterns.* New York: Wiley, 1962, pp. 455–467.

Craddick, R. A., and Leipold, W. D. Note on the height of draw-a-person figures by male alcoholics. *J Proj Tech* 32:486, 1968.

Dinkmeyer, D. D., and Muro, J. J. *Group Counseling: Theory and Practice.* Itasca, Ill.: Peacock, 1971.

Fenichel, O. *The Psychoanalytic Theory of Neurosis.* New York: Norton, 1945, p. 27.

Gross, W. R., and Adler, L. O. Aspects of alcoholics' self-concepts as measured by the Tennessee Self-Concept Scale. *Psychol Rep* 27:431–434, 1970.

Guttmacher, J. A., and Birk, L. Group therapy: What specific therapeutic advantages? *Comprehen Psychiat* 12:546–556, 1971.

Hansen, J. C., Warner, R. W., and Smith, E. M. *Group Counseling: Theory and Process.* Chicago: Rand-McNally, 1976, p. 259.

Harris, T. A. *I'm O.K., You're O.K.: A Practical Guide to Transactional Analysis.* New York: Harper & Row, 1969.

Konovsky, M., and Wilsnack, S. C. Social drinking and self-esteem in married couples. *J Stud Alc* 43:319–333, 1982.

Mahler, C. A. *Group Counseling in the Schools.* Boston: Houghton Mifflin, 1969.

Maslow, A. *Motivation and Personality,* 2nd ed. New York: Harper & Row, 1970.

Ohlsen, M. M. *Group Counseling.* New York: Holt, Rinehart & Winston, 1970.

Rogers, C. R., *On Becoming a Person: A Therapist's View of Psychotherapy.* Boston: Houghton Mifflin, 1961.

Stokes, J. P. Toward an understanding of cohesion in personal change groups. *Int J Psychol* 33(4):449–467, 1983.

Trotzer, J. P. Group counseling: Process and perspective. Guidelines for pupil services. Madison: Wisconsin Department of Public Instruction, 1972, vol. 10, pp. 105–110.

Wolf, A., and Schwartz, E. K. *Psychoanalysis in Groups.* New York: Grune & Stratton, 1962.

Suggested Readings on Psychoanalytic Groups

Becker, B. J. The psychodynamics of analytic group psychotherapy. *Am J Psychoanal,* 32:177–185, 1972.

Brill, A. A. *Basic Principles of Psychoanalysis.* Garden City, N.Y.: Doubleday, 1949.

Dreikurs, R. Group psychotherapy and group approaches: The collected papers of Rudolf Dreikurs. The Alfred Adler Institute of Chicago, 1960.

Fowlkes, S. H. and Anthony, E. J. *Group Psychotherapy: Psychoanalytic Approach,* 2nd ed. Baltimore, Md.: Penquin Books, 1965.

Freud, S. *An Outline of Psychoanalysis* New York: Norton, 1949.

Goldman, G. D. Some applications of Harry Stack Sullivans theories to group psychotherapy. *Int J Group Psychother* 7:385–391, 1957.

Horney, J. Values and problems of group psychoanalysis. *Am J Psychoanal* 12:80–81, 1952.

Meninger, J. *Theory of Psychoanalytic Technique.* New York: Basic Books, 1958.

Slavson, S. R. *A Textbook in Analytic Group Psychotherapy.* New York: International Universities Press, 1964.

Wolf, A. The psychoanalysis of groups. In H. M. Ruitenbeek (ed), *Group Therapy Today.* Chicago: Aldine-Atherton, pp. 67–96, 1969.

Yalom, I. D. *Theory of Group Psychotherapy,* New York: Basic Books, 1970.

Suggested Readings on Encounter Groups

Blanchard, W. H. Encounter group and society. In R. N. Solomon and B. B.

Berzon (eds), *New Perspectives on Encounter Groups.* San Francisco: Jossey-Bass, 1972, pp. 13–29.

Burton, A. Encounter, existence and psychotherapy. In A. Burton (Ed), *Encounter: The Theory and Practice of Encounter Groups.* San Francisco: Jossey-Bass, 1969, pp. 7–26.

Coulson, W. Inside a basic encounter group. *T Counseling Psychol* 2:1–27, 1970.

Rogers, C. R. The process of the basic encounter groups. In J. F. G. Bugental (ed.), *Challenges of Humanistic Psychology.* New York: McGraw-Hill, 1967, pp. 267–277.

Stoller, F. H. A stage for trust. In A. Burton (ed.), *Encounter: The Theory and Practice of Encounter Groups,* San Francisco: Jossey-Bass, 1969, pp. 81–96.

Thomas, H. F. Encounter, the game of no game. In A. Burton (ed), *Encounter: The Theory and Practice of Encounter Groups.* San Francisco: Jossey-Bass, 1969, pp. 69–80.

Suggested Readings on Gestalt Groups

Levitsky, A., and Simkin, J. S. Gestalt therapy. In L. N. Soloman and B. Berzon (eds.), *New Perspective on Encounter Groups.* San Francisco: Jossey-Bass, 1972, pp. 245–254.

Massarik F. Standards for group leadership. In R. N. Soloman and B. Berzon (eds.), *New Perspectives on Encounter Groups.* San Francisco: Jossey-Bass, 1972, pp. 68–82.

Perls, F. S., Heffeline, R. F., and Goodman, P. *Gestalt Therapy.* New York: Julian Press, 1951 (paperback, Dell, 1965).

Perls, F. S. *Gestalt Therapy Verbatim.* Lafayette, Calif.: Real People Press, 1969 (paperback, Bantam, 1971).

Perls, L. One Gestalt therapist's approach. In J. Fagan and I. L. Shephard (eds.), *Gestalt Therapy Now.* Palo Alto, Calif.: Science and Behavior Books, 1970, pp. 120–130.

Polstel, E., and Polstel, M. *Gestalt Therapy Integrated,* New York: Brunner/Mazel, 1973.

Suggested Readings on Transactional Analysis Groups

Berne, E. *Transactional Analysis in Psychotherapy.* New York: Grove Press, 1961.

Berne, E. *Principles of Group Treatment.* New York: Oxford University Press, 1966.

Dusay, J., and Steiner, C. Transactional analysis in groups. In H. I. Kaplan and B. J. Sacock (eds.), *Comprehensive Group Psychotherapy*. Baltimore, Md.: Williams & Wilkins, 1971, pp. 198–240.

Harris, T. A. *I'm O.K., You're O.K.: A Practical Guide to Transactional Analysis*. New York: Harper & Row, 1969.

Holland, G. Transactional analysis. In R. Corsini (ed.), *Current Psychotherapies*. Itasca, Ill.: Peacock, 1973, pp. 353–399.

Chapter II

Personality of the Alcoholic Group

Every alcoholic counseling group is different. Each has its own personality. With the addition of a new member, that personality changes. It changes too with the dropout or termination of a member. The alcoholic group personality can be understood as unique and dynamic, and as a blend of the individual personalities involved.

As a counselor the author has learned that alcoholic groups have certain commonalities that set them apart from the personalities of non-alcoholic groups. This chapter addresses these commonalities.

PERCEPTION

PERCEPTION is the axis upon which our personality turns. The interpersonal competence and general health of humans are dependent upon the quality of our perception. How we perceive people will determine how we interact with them. If our perception of others is generally accurate, we usually find our interactions rewarding, or at least predictable. If our perception of others is distorted, we tend to find our interactions unsatisfying, and often punishing. In short how we relate to others and what we get out of our relationships are in large part based on our perceptions.

To be effective it is important that the group counselor have a full appreciation of just how distorted the alcoholic perception of self and others really is. Group counselors who are themselves recovering alcoholics seem to have an edge in this. The research findings that follow should contribute to that appreciation.

The evidence is that alcoholics do not perceive themselves or others the way nonalcoholics do. Normal, healthy adults differentiate between people and the physical environment. Alcoholics do not. Too often alcoholics suffer from *perceptual generalization.* People and settings blend emotionally for them. When hospitalized they often cannot discriminate among hospital room, doctor, medical equipment, and nurses. In the alcoholic's view, they are the same because they all have contributed to making the alcoholic *dependent* on the hospital institution. (Witkin et al., 1962).

These feelings of being dependent are very much a part of the distorted alcoholic perception of the world (Karp et al., 1963; Goldstein & Chotlos, 1963; Chess et al., 1971) and explain in considerable measure why so many alcoholics have surrendered to their environment, why they feel victimized.

The surrender and sense of victimization are complemented and compounded by the view that alcoholics have of themselves. Two researchers in studies done separately found that alcoholic men when asked to draw a person were not as likely as nonalcoholics to draw a man first (Wisotsky, 1958; Laird, 1962). The conclusion is that alcoholics do not take much pride in their bodies, or in their persons. Perhaps it is because they do not view their own bodies as favorably as they do the women's bodies. Or they might perceive women as dominating, controlling, or more important. These are interpretations, and thus are subjective and open to question. What is unquestionable, however, is that alcoholics take a demeaning view of their bodies.

There is evidence that suggests that alcoholics are physiologically more sensitive to pain and perceive it with more anxiety then do nonalcoholics (Petrie, 1967). There is even more evidence that alcohol miitgates pain more in alcoholics then in nonalcoholics (Barnes, 1980; Cutter & Fisher, 1980; Buchsbaum & Ludwig, 1981). These studies suggest that perception is indeed a critical factor in the development of the alcoholic disease.

DEFENSES

DEFENSES may be understood as emotional responses to a perceived threat. They are important for at least two reasons—they feed egos and they defend them from threat, either actual or felt.

Healthy people use defenses to help them perceive other people, situations, and events selectively, that is, with more satisfaction, or at least with less threat. Defenses, then, can and do promote psychological health. By using defenses people are able to develop relationships that enhance their lives.

Among alcoholics this very necessary process of defense becomes pathological. Their perception of both self and others is distorted. Their emotional responses to distortions often are confused, inappropriately suspicious, and/or unnecessarily fearful. The alcoholics' submissiveness to environment, constant, latent sense of victimization, deep hostility, and inability to maintain and promote enhancing relationships can be understood better within this context of a weak, ineffective defense structure.

To be effective the group counselor both must understand and be able to respond to the defenses of the group. Indeed a major task of the counselor is to help the group members restructure defense systems in a way that will facilitate a more accurate and healthier perception of both themselves and others. This process of restructuring is an integral part of the group interactions. Group progress, the counselor should understand, complements and is a function of defense restructuring. To put it another way, a counselor who does not feel the group is making progress should look more closely at the group members' defenses. The author's experience is that the obstacles to group progress are usually there.

Only those defenses most commonly found among alcoholic group members will be treated here.

1. Denial.

2. Displacement.

3. Fantasy.

4. Projection.
5. Rationalization.
6. Intellectualization.
7. Regression.
8. Repression.
9. Sublimation.

Defenses are unconscious. When defensive, group members ordinarily are not aware that they are so. (The possible exception for the healthier members might be when they use rationalization.) What this means is that defensive members are quite unaware of their fears, hostilities, and suspicions.

Although examined and explained individually here, the reader should know that defenses operate more commonly in tandem or in support of another defense. Thus the alcoholic who denies the disease often uses rationalization and/or projection to maintain and support that denial.

Denial

Denial is the refusal to admit to one's condition or behavior. An example of this in the group are the members who continue to imbibe secretly (they "know" they have it under control). When questioned by a suspicious peer member about their drinking, they may respond with jokes, anger, or questions of their own. The insidious part is that when they are responding, they are themselves at a loss as to the why of their response.

Note: This is the prime defense among the seven destructive behaviors (see Chapter III).

Displacement

Displacement ordinarily refers to the ventilation of hostility toward a person or persons who do not warrant it. In the alcoholic group, especially in the early acclimation stages, this is fairly common behavior with new members. The engendering agent for the hostility, however, may well be not another person but rather the conflict and consequent anxiety precipitated by trying to achieve sobriety. The most common examples of displacement in groups are the verbal harassment, hounding, and belittling of another member. The author's experience is that the scapegoat is usually the one who qualifies as the "most" of some kind—pretentious, intellectual, submissive, casual, wealthy. The only requirement is that the person stand out. To the very sensitive eye of the alcoholic, practiced in displacement, immediately fixing on this person is not hard.

The displacement defense does little to promote a healthier climate in the group. It blocks rather than facilitates communication. At the same time, it does provide a release for hostility and frustration. And it does more. It furnishes the scapegoats of the group with an opportunity to learn why they are so and it allows the member(s) who use displacement to see that this defense does little to enhance others or themselves.

Note: Typical behaviors associated with displacement include silence, antagonism, and assaulting.

Fantasy

Daydreaming, or fantasy, is usually the defense and constant solace of the quiet, inhibited, nonparticipatory member. Many group members condition themselves by using alcohol to find more reward in fantasy than in interaction. With the help of liquor, they are able to achieve what they never had achieved or felt they could; namely, fulfillment of their wishes and/or a sense of power and control over their environment (McClelland et al., 1972). What the counselor should understand, then, is that group interaction is more threatening for the member who continues to hold fantasy as a prime defense in his or her emotional repertoire. This is a defense that usually feeds the closet drinker; it is not an easy one to spot in groups. The alcoholic for whom fantasy is a prime destructive defense, may be expansive, warm, and positively gregarious in group. Such a person might also be shy and inhibited. With this in mind, it could be advisable for the counselor to schedule and structure an occasional session where group members are encouraged to discuss their fantasies. The author's experience is that groups have found such sessions very profitable.

Note: Among typical behaviors associated with fantasy are antagonizing, manipulating, housekeeping, clowning, and professionalizing. When combined with sublimation, fantasy can also effect enhancing behaviors.

Projection

To attribute to others the motives and feelings that one harbors oneself is called projection. This defense finds fertile ground in the person whose interpersonal relations have become debilitated by distancing and/or a lack of contact with people. The alcoholic is just such a person. In the group this defense is most evident in a member's suspiciousness, sharp temper, and too-quick-to-take-offense attitude. Additional manifestations of projection are reflected in a member's oblique questioning of the counselor or of other members. An inability to tolerate whispering by others and constant interpersonal evasiveness might also be signs of the projection defense.

This defense is especially insidious in the group because it works against the development of trust. Projection fosters suspiciousness. Openness and candor by the counselor and other members seem to be most effective antidotes.

Note: Behaviors associated with this defense include antagonizing, manipulating, and assaulting.

Rationalization

People use rationalization when they try to justify actual or felt inadequacies or behaviors. Among alocholics this defense is frequently used in tandem with denial to support continued drinking; that is, "I'm not all that sure that I ever really was an alcoholic. I mean like I'd go a week, two sometimes, before I drank." What the counselor should focus on in such typical and transparent rationalizations is the alcoholic's present need to redefine the past in order to justify future drinking. If the group were to ignore such a comment (usually it does not), the counselor should not do so. The perceptive counselor makes use of rationalizations for group discussion and exploration.

Intellectualization

When alcoholics employ this defense, they use their mental competencies and ignore their feelings. They use only their minds to relate to people, situations, events, and problems. Intellectualizers are usually intelligent and articulate and have a strong penchant for analysis and explanation. Their problem is that they behave as if they have no feeling. Sometimes they honestly and consciously believe that. They never learned how to communicate feelings. Typically they do not know how to share them appropriately or how to accept them. Thus they ordinarily relate to others with long, unemotional, dull speeches. Their lack of emotionality makes it difficult, almost impossible, to build meaningful long-term relationships.

In the alcoholic group, the intellectualization defense can be manifested in two very different personalities. The quiet, inhibited, and shy individuals who find it very painful to talk and to share are one type. Most of what they say is thoughtful and meaningful. Perceptive counselors can and should reward the spare utterings of these intellectualizers. The other personality operates at the other end of the interactive continuum. Once started these individuals seem quite unable to stop talking. Often they are unaware that they are monopolizing and dominating the discussion. Both types seek the same end—to relate and get close to others in the group. If counselors bear this in mind, they can facilitate achievement of that end.

Note: Behaviors associated with this defense are silence, absence, housekeeping, and professionalizing. Intellectualization can also effect enhancing behaviors. (See "sublimation".)

Regression is the defense of the individual who behaves in a way that is more common in children. In the alcoholic group, this defense is exemplified by temper tantrums, pouting, or sulking. These behaviors jibe well with the common alcoholic tendency for manipulation. Therefore, the astute counselor never permits a member to reward regressive behavior by a peer member.

Repression

People repress by letting the memory of a trauma slip into their unconscious. Thus the person or situation related to the event is forgotten. The anxiety associated with the trauma is also forgotten. The anxiety, however, can be triggered by a word, a look, a passing tableau that the individual unconsciously feels is a part of the original trauma. The most insidious aspect of all this is that individuals have no idea why they feel the anxiety. Repression can rightfully be understood to be an emotionally debilitating defense. Tahka (1966), after much study, concluded that alcoholics repress much more than do nonalcoholics.

As noted in Chapter I, a focal point of psychoanalytic counseling is to encourage group members to free associate in order to uncover the repression. For a group such a process can seem interminable.

The view here is that it is important to understand the nature of repressions but it is not important to treat them as exclusive and specific entities. Repressions are aspects of the alcoholic's personality to be dealt with only if the alcoholic feels and expresses the need to do so; that is, that it is important to other aspects of the individual's total life.

This conselor's experience has been that the disease of alcoholism cannot be treated efficiently or effectively in the group if it is viewed as an exclusive function of childhood repression. Treatment seems to be more successful when it is geared to the whole person rather than focusing on a single defense and attributing to it the major cause of the disease.

Sublimation

When alcoholics sublimate they channel their need to drink in a socially productive way. Thus the energy that they might have employed in a destructive way (drinking) is emotionally invested in enhancing behaviors. In group such behaviors include trusting, facilitating, giving feedback, listening, and communicating.

When combined with sublimation, other defenses that are used destructively by the alcoholic can become enhancing. Most notable among these are fantasy and intellectualization.

Once alcoholics stop drinking, they develop many ideas and feelings about their new self-images, about who they will be, what they will be, and how they will operate. Fantasy plays a critical part in all of this. Before they can effectively sublimate in group, they have to fantasize about it. Fantasy can be, and often is, a springboard for sublimation.

Intellectualization can also play an important part in the enhancing behaviors. In group good listeners must be dispassionate listeners. Similarly, feedback must be delivered clearly and articulately to be effective.

In sum, the sublimation defense plays an important role in the alcoholic's recovery. This is especially true when it is combined with fantasy and intellectualization.

CONSCIENCE

CONSCIENCE is an integral part of our personality. We cannot function healthily without it. It is that little bit of society we have made a part of ourselves.

Without conscience we cannot trust and we cannot love. Without conscience we become narcissistic,—concerned exclusively with self. In the narcissist's view others exist to be manipulated and to serve. Narcissists who have no conscience have been termed psychopaths. There are elements of the psychopath in the alcoholic who continues to drink. Thus when under the influence, alcoholics function without conscience. They can lie, cheat, steal, and abuse even their families without remorse. Their thoughts and energy are directed toward themselves only—toward maintaining the "buzzlike high."

When alcoholics return to a sober state, conscience returns—and not uncommonly in an overly scrupulous form. In this state individuals function at the other end of the conscience continuum. Indeed conscience takes over the personality, and when it does, decisions are not made by the ego—that is, out of choice—but are made out of guilt by an overcompensating conscience. When in this state, individuals are wracked by guilt. The return to liquor by many alcoholics is motivated by the need to anesthesize the conscience.

A number of studies have been made that show that the alcoholic's conscience is not as well developed as that of someone from the normative population (Goss & Morosko,1969; Kristianson, 1970; Spiegel et al., 1970). Complementing this lack of development is a strong, depressive quality found in many alcoholic personalities.

Hoffman (1970) found that alcoholics are more depressed than nonalcoholics. What this means is that alcoholics have trouble establishing goals and persevering in their attainment. The depression in group sessions can be displayed in a variety of ways. The most common are in rationalizations about procrastination, in displacements on other group members, and in apparent lack of interest in group activities.

The depressive state is a phenomenon with which the alcoholic group must deal regularly. It is understandable. If they are nothing else, alcoholics are very tired people—tired of the latent but constant emotional conflict between a nonexistent and an overly scrupulous conscience. In addition most alcoholics, especially in their depressive states, recognize that many of the decisions that they made while reacting to an excessive conscience were self-defeating, socially inappropriate, or just plain foolish. Such recognition fuels the alcoholic's depressive state. Such a state sets the stage for the phenomenon termed BUD—building up to drink. There are signs of this while in group that should be recognized.

1. Sudden, unexplained periods of silence by usually cheerful, talkative participants.
2. Over confident, unrealistic talk by clients about how they are going to adhere to their sobriety.
3. A sudden injection of absolutes—always, never, and rigid; unasked-for resolutions about maintenance of sobriety.
4. Long monologs characterized primarily by gloomy, depressed talk.
5. An apathetic and listless appearance for no apparent reason.
6. Sudden use of evasiveness by a usually open type of person.
7. Hypomanic behavior and talk by a usually deliberate, slow-moving, slow-talking member.

RESEARCH FINDINGS

THIS AUTHOR pre- and posttested 32 alcoholics with the Rorschach and the Thematic Apperception tests to assess the effect of the group counseling experience. Twenty-two of the subjects were men; ten were women. All the subjects were middle-class. Twenty-six were employed. Three of the unemployed were women who chose to stay home with young children. No more than four of the subjects belonged to the same group. The 32 were distributed among ten different groups. None of the subjects were in counseling for more than four months. The author was counselor for two groups in which the subjects were participants.

Pretest Findings

The pretest findings by the subjects showed:

1. A high expectation to be rejected.
2. An introverted orientation.
3. A high degree of hostility.
4. An inordinate use of projection defense.
5. A low self-esteem.

The subjects' basic understanding was that people would not like them; they expected to be rejected. The emotional distancing so characteristic of the alcoholic can be understood better in view of this interpersonal stance.

There are still many who believe that alcoholics are basically gregarious and outgoing, and prefer being with others to being alone. None of the individuals in this sample were like that. They were all turned in on themselves. Their degree of introversion ranged from a depressed, brooding view of self and the world to an intellectualized reflective and meditative disposition. These people found thought and self more rewarding than talk and others.

While the author expected to find hostility, he did not expect to find such a great amount and for it to be so all-inclusive. It ranged from a crude, thick, surface veneer to a well-disguised, sophisticated indignation. But it was always there and plentiful. In many of the cases, this hostility stemmed from the alcoholics' victimization syndrome. Some felt they had been emotionally short-changed, some intensely resented the physical abuse they had experienced during childhood (two of the women had been sexually molested as children). Others were furious that they were crippled by their drinking. The author felt that this last anger was the healthiest. Given the proper counselor direction, he saw it as a first step, an excellent springboard to recovery.

Not unsurprisingly this inordinate degree of anger resulted in a prodigious use of the projection defense. Indeed this was the primary defense of 17 of the subjects and a factor in the defense structure of all except three. Projection is self-destructive interpersonally. It is the defense of those who perceive a hostile, threatening world. Such a perception usually begets a response in kind. The result is predictable—a lack in relationships and a life of aloneness.

A low self-esteem among the subjects was the last major finding in the pretesting. The author was not surprised as he had learned early in his work with alcoholics that this is the most common denominator among them (Perez, 1985).

The importance of self-esteem cannot be overstated. It is the foundation upon which personality is built. It is the foundation upon which all human performance is premised. Simply stated, if we feel we are good, we perform well. Conversely, if we feel we are unworthy, we perform badly—or we do not perform at all.

The finding of a low self-esteem is perfectly consistent with the other four findings: a high expectation to be rejected, an introverted orientation, a hostile perception, and the projection defense.

Other researchers also have found a correlation between alcoholic drinking and a low self-esteem (Segal et al., 1980). A low self-esteem among alcoholics is invariably associated with a distorted, idealized image. The considerable disparity between the two leads to intense dissatisfaction with self and a relapse into liquor. (Eastman & Norris, 1982). And this is apparently an even more acute problem for women than for men. Beckman (1978), for example, found that in general female alcoholics have a lower self-esteem than do male alcoholics.

Posttest Findings

In examining the posttest protocols, the author sought to interpret and relate the findings to the pretest results. This proved difficult in some cases because the subjects' perceptions in posttesting were so radically different from those that they reported in the first testing.

The results showed:

1. A diminuition in feelings of rejection.
2. A continuation of introversion but of a healthier quality.
3. A reduction in hostility.
4. Less use of the projection defense, which in some measure had been replaced by sublimation.
5. A rise in self-esteem.

The expectation of rejection lingered but was not nearly as strong, and in some cases had moved toward a realistic, even healthier view of others. There is little doubt that the forced interaction of group counseling in most cases pierced the isolation shell behind which most of the participants had been hiding (in one case for over 12 years). In every case but three, the subjects' Rorschach interpretations indicated a tendency (in a few cases a strong one) to be attracted toward the emotions and feelings of others.

The tendency to introversion continued. However, the brooding-like depressive quality had to a large extent evaporated. The reflective, meditative quality remained fairly intact. The author did not interpret this as unhealthy. If one thinks about it, alcoholics who are honestly resolved to maintain their sobriety could not do so if they did not retain a strong penchant toward introversion.

The crude veneers of hostility had been thinned considerably by the counseling. The sophisticated indignation had abated but was still evident. There is little doubt that the warmth and sharing experiences of the group had made a very positive impact upon all the members. It should be noted, however, that the four months of counseling had not eradicated the hostility in any of the participants. All of them still harbored feelings of anger toward people in their past. The difference, and an important one, was that now the anger was felt and directed specifically toward those who had engendered it. It was *not* unfocused and generalized.

The projection defense had been greatly diminished in every subject. The candor and authenticity of the group had had a positive impact. While none of the subjects had developed an overly optimistic view of others or of their own competencies, the hostile, threatening perception of the world that the subjects had held prior to the counseling had diminished in intensity. The reduced use of projection was compensated for in considerable measure by the development of sublimation. Thus as participants developed a more positive view of themselves and others, they began to think and do for others and they began to find reward in such thought and activity.

The slow but pronounced movement toward sublimation was in large part a function of the rise in self-esteem. As they shared, self-disclosed, and became involved in peer members' problems, the participants began to feel worthier. Some began to feel for the first time that they had something to contribute, and they liked the feeling.

THE ALCOHOLIC FAMILY

Research Findings

The evidence is that alcoholism is learned in the family. McKenna and Pickens (1981) found that when both parents are alcoholic, a child is more likely to become so than if only one were. In addition, they found that if one parent was alcoholic, then there is a greater probability that the child will become alcoholic than if neither parent were. What this study shows is that alcoholism in the family is a family problem, not an individual one. In the alcoholic family, children are emotionally deprived, and at least one study shows that the deprivation seems to have a more negative impact upon girls growing up than upon boys (Beckman et al., 1980).

It is the children of alcoholics, the developing child and adolescent, for whom the effects of alcohol are especially destructive. A disproportionate number of these adolescents move into adulthood without having experienced adolescence. They experience their first intoxication sooner than other children and are more likely to have to enter alcoholism treatment (McKenna & Pickens, 1981). Though they interact with parents, socialize with peers, and sit in classrooms, they learn nothing because they move in an alcoholic haze. The buzz that they cultivate does not permit them to learn about family living, to acquire social skills, or achieve academically. Insulated by the buzz, they escape all the normal anxieties, pains, and frustrations of living. They live in a synthetic, plastic world created by liquor. They enter adulthood equipped with the emotional and social competencies of children (Milman et al., 1983).

Research shows that family groups have self-esteem just as do individuals. And alcoholic families have lower self-esteems than do nonalcoholic families (McKenna & Pickents, 1983). The evidence is strong that ingestion of alcohol has a debilitating effect upon the family. One study indicates that the self-esteem of married couples declines in direct proportion to the increase in alcohol consumption (Konovsky & Wilsnack, 1982).

What all these studies point up is that the family is a group and can be infected as such. The position here is that the infection can be treated within the family context. Family counseling* not only is viable, but is a highly desirable treatment approach for the family diseased by alcoholism. All the material presented thus far is as applicable to counseling the family as it is to any alcoholic group because a family that harbors an alcoholic member can be rightfully termed an alcoholic group, and as such is in dire need of counseling. What this counselor has learned is that an alcoholic's disease may well be a symptom of important familial problems.

As noted, the family is a group, but it is a group unto itself. Familial dynamics are indigenous to a family and in important ways unlike those of any other group. In a previously published work (Perez, 1979), this author pointed out that effective family counseling must proceed on certain premises. He has found that these premises can be adapted quite nicely to the alcoholic family.

1. The alcoholic's illness comes not from the individual alone but from intrafamilial interaction.

2. One or more members of the family profit psychologically from the alcoholic's illness. A corollary of these assumptions is that the alcoholic is not the lone member of the family with problems.

3. The family that continues in therapy demonstrates a positive need to improve its health.

4. The parental relationship is a critical factor in how family counseling will proceed.

*A list of recommended reading on family counseling is included at the end of this chapter.

These four premises are derived from the idea that a family, like any functioning group, operates as a unit. In such a unit, each person has a role (understood by all the others) and interacts in that role. So long as members play their understood roles, the family maintains its equilibrium, its "homeostatic balance" (Jackson, 1957). What should be noted here is that the homeostatic balance maintained is not necessarily a healthy one. Unfortunately, family members often play their roles and use up their energy to contribute to the maintenance of a sick homeostasis. The best illustrations of this, of course, are the members of an alcoholic family.

The leading actor in the drama of familial alcoholism is not the alcoholic, usually termed the IP (identified patient). The leading actor is the enabler.

The Enabler

The enabler can be a parent, spouse, or child. There are as many different personalities among enablers as there are enablers. At the same time, there is one quality that is essential to enablers. This is overprotectiveness.

Enablers have a perception comparable to that of overprotective parents. The latter's basic problem is that they are blind to the fact that the child is a separate and distinct human being with an ego who must learn to make his or her own decisions if he or she is ever going to be independent and healthy. In their zeal to protect such children, parents attempt to function as the child's ego. They do not hold the child accountable or responsible for any acts. Their intent, consciously or unconsciously, is to turn the child into an overdevoted companion.

The enabler operates with a comparable perception and motive. With an enabler type in the family, alcoholics can regress comfortably into childhood. They do not have to be responsible or accountable, and the enabler protects, defends, and often even buys the liquor, sometimes under protest, but buys it.

Why do enablers "enable"? The constant, acutely profound need of enablers is to be needed, or more accurately, to be loved. This author's work with enablers has led him to believe that there is still another need here—a constant, latent terror that ultimately they will be left alone.

Whatever the motive, enablers see their function as one of insulating the alcoholic from pain and shame, and accountability. The eternal frustration for enablers is that instead of gratitude and devotion, the alcoholic responds with abuse and condemnation. The problem, of course, is that the enablers' self-motives prevent them from seeing the guilt and consequent hostility they inspire in the alcoholic.

Goals

The first concern of the group counselor is to find out who the enabler is. This is easy. What is not easy is to help the enabler (sometimes there is more than one) to come to appreciate how he or she is part of the problem. There are two basic goals within the process of therapy with the alcoholic family:

1. To bring all the members to the realization that alcoholism is a familial problem, not the IP's alone.
2. To help all members realize that a healthier homeostasis can be achieved only if the enabler, the alcoholic and others involved can confront and come to appreciate each other's perceptions, expectations, and interactions.

SUMMARY

ALCOHOLIC GROUPS have certain commonalities that set them apart from nonalcoholic groups. Chief among these is a distorted perception that is conducive to poor or nonexistent relationships.

Alcoholic perception is characterized by perceptual generalization, dependency, a sense of victimization, a demeaning self-view, and an exquisite sensitivity to pain.

Defenses may be understood as emotional responses to perceived threat. Those that concern the group counselor most are denial, displacement, fantasy, projection, rationalization, intellectualization, regression, repression, and sublimation.

Conscience is a critical factor in personality and in the alcoholic it fluctuates between being nonexistent and being overscrupulous. This fluctuation can, and often does, lead to a depressive state in the alcoholic and a factor that needs to be dealt with in group. The depressive state, in turn, can lead to the BUD phenomenon.

Pretesting of group subjects showed: (1) a high expectation to be rejected; (2) an introverted orientation; (3) a high degree of hostility; (4) an inordinate use of the projection defense; and (5) a low self-esteem. The posttest findings showed: (1) a diminuition in feelings of rejection; (2) a continuation in introversion but of a healthier quality; (3) a reduction in hostility; (4) a reduction in projection and some use of sublimation; and (5) a rise in self-esteem.

The research evidence is that alcoholism is learned in the family, has an especially destructive effect upon the children of alcoholics, and invariably diminishes the family's self-esteem. Family counseling with alcoholics needs to proceed on the basis of clearly defined premises. These are derived from the idea that a family, like any functioning group, operates as a unit to maintain its homeostatic balance. Sometimes, as in the alcoholic family, this balance becomes unhealthy. A major reason for this is the role played by the enabler. The counselor's first concern is to find out who the enabler is and then to help him or her appreciate how alcoholism is a familial problem. A healthier homeostasis is not possible until all the members can appreciate this fact.

REFERENCES

Barnes, G. E. Characteristics of the clinical alcoholic personality. *J Stud Alc* 41:894–909, 1980.

Beckman, L. J. The self-esteem of alcoholic women. *J Stud Alc* 39:491–498, 1978.

Beckman, L. J., Day T., Bardsley, P., and Seeman, A. Z. The personality characteristics and Family backgrounds of women alcoholics. *Int J Addict* 15:147–54, 1980.

Buchsbaum, M. S., and Ludwig, A. M. Effects of sensory input and alcohol administration on visual evoked potentials in normal subjects and alcoholics. In H. Begletter, (ed.), *Alcohol Intoxication and Withdrawal*, Vol. 4, New York: Plenum Press, 1981.

Chess, S. B., Neuringer, C., and Goldstein, G. Arousal and field dependency in alcoholics. J Gen Psychol 85:93–102, 1971.

Cutter, H. S. G., and Fisher, J. C. Family experience and the motives for drinking. *Int J Addict* 15:339–358, 1980.

Eastman, C., and Norris, H. Alcohol dependence, relapse and self-identity. *J Stud Alc* 43:1214–1231, 1982.

Goldstein, G., and Chotlos, J. W. Dependency and brain damage in alcoholics *Percept M of Skills* 21:135–150, 1965.

Goss, A., and Morosko, T. E. Alcoholism and clinical symptons. *J Abnorm Psychol* 74:682–684, 1969.

Hoffman, H. Personality characteristics of alcoholics in relation to age. *Psychol Rep* 27:167–171,1970.

Jackson, D. The question of family homeostasis: *Psychiat Qu Suppl* 31:79–90,1957.

Karp, S. A., Poster, D. C., and Goodman, A. Differentiation in alcoholic women. *J Personality* 31:386–393, 1963.

Konovsky, M., and Wilsnack, S. C. Social drinking and self-esteem in married couples. *J Stud Alc* 43:319–333, 1982.

Kristianson, P. A. A comparison study of two alcoholic groups and a control group. *Br J Med Psychol* 43:161–175, 1970.

Laird, J. T. A comparison of male normals, psychiatric patients and alcoholics for sex drawn first. *J Clin Psychol* 18:302, 1962.

McClelland, D. C., Warner, E., and Vanneman, R. Drinking in the wider context of restrained and unrestrained assertive thoughts and acts. In D. C. McClellend, W. N. Davis, R. Kalin: and E. Wanner *The Drinking Man*. New York: Free Press, 1972.

McKenna, T., and Pickens, R. Alcoholic children of alcoholics, *J Stud Alc* 42:1021–1029, 1981.

McKenna, T., and Pickens, R. Personality characteristics of alcoholic children of alcoholics. *J Stud Alc* 44(4), 1983.

Milman, D. H., Bennett, A. A., and Hanson, M. Psychological effects of alcohol in children and adolescents—alcohol health and research. World National Institute on Alcohol Abuse and Alcoholism, Vol. 7 No. 4, 1983.

Perez, J. F. *Family Counseling: Theory and Practice*. New York: Van Nostrand, 1979.

Perez, J. F. *Counseling the Alcoholic*. Munice, Ind.: Accelerated Development, 1985.

Petrie, A. *Individuality in Pain and Suffering*, Chicago: University of Chicago Press, 1967.

Segal, B., Huba, G. J., and Singer, J. L. Reasons for drug and alcohol use by college students. *Inst J Addict* 15:489–498, 1980.

Spiegel, D., Hadley, P. A., and Hadley, R. G. Personality test patterns of rehabilitation center alcoholics, psychiatric inpatients and normals. *J Clin Psychol* 26:366–371, 1970.

Tahka, V. The alcoholic personality; A clinical study. Finnish Foundation for Alcohol Studies Publisher No. 13, Helsinki, 1966.

Witkin, H. A., Dyk, R. B., Faterson, H. F., Goodenough, D. R., and Karp, S. A. *Psychological Differentiation*. New York: Wiley, 1962.

Wisotsky, M. A note on the order of figure drawing among incarcerated alcoholics. *J Clin Psychol* 15:65, 1958.

Suggested Readings on Family Counseling

Blich, D. A. *Techniques of Family Psychotherapy, A Primer*. New York: Grune & Stratton, 1973.

Euchson, G. D., and Hogan, T. P. *Family Therapy, An Introduction to Theory and Technique*. Monterey, Calif.: Brooks/Cole, 1972.

Haley, J. *Changing Families, A Family Therapy Reader*. New York: Grune & Stratton, 1971.

Howells, J. G. *Theory and Practice of Family Psychiatry*. New York: Brunner/Mazel, 1971.

Minuchin, S. *Families and Family Therapy*. Cambridge, Mass.: Harvard University Press, 1974.

Perez, J. F. *Family Counseling: Theory and Practice*. New York: Van Nostrand, 1979.

Satir, V. *Conjoint Family Therapy*. Palo Alto, Calif.: Science and Behavior Books, 1967.

Chapter III

The Group Member—*Behaviors*

Every group session with alcoholics is human theater. There is poignant drama, melodrama in abundance, comedy, and, not uncommonly, tragedy. Alcoholics, perhaps because of their tendency to introspection, are sensitive to all of it. The behaviors and the consequent feelings expressed are broad in spectrum and they are the raw data with which the counselor works to help members achieve and maintain recovery. The three types of behavior most commonly found in an alcoholic group can be categorized under three headings.

1. Destructive behaviors.
2. Enhancing behaviors.
3. Affective behaviors.

DESTRUCTIVE BEHAVIORS

THE PRIME characteristic of those afflicted with alcoholism is destructiveness. Destructiveness in alcoholics can best be understood as a function of resistance. Originally a psychoanalytic term (see Chapter I), the concept can be adapted nicely to help understand the alcoholic in group.

Thus one psychoanalyst's definition of resistance could be a description of the behavior of alcoholics in group counseling. Resistance, Becker (1972) wrote, is "basically a clinging to existing, destructive patterns rather than moving on to new, constructive orientations in living" (p. 181).

This clinging to destructive patterns by alcoholics is especially apparent in the initial stages of the group, before rapport, cohesion, and a sense of identification develop among the members. The counselor should be aware that with the development of these resistance is not necessarily alleviated, but may only be going underground. When that happens the alcoholics's behaviors do not become less destructive, but become more sophisticated and harder for the leader to deal with. For example, where a member's withdrawal was characterized by muteness, he or she now may exchange simple pleasantries without getting any closer to the leader or the group. Thus although no longer mute, the member is still just as withdrawn from the group.

Destructive behaviors can be evinced in a variety of forms. The following are the ones most in evidence in the alcoholic group.

1. Absence.
2. Silence.
3. Antagonism.
4. Manipulation.
5. Housekeeping.
6. Clowning.
7. Professionalizing.

Absence

Absence from the group classically illustrates the prime defense of the alcoholic—denial. The rationale, conscious or unconscious, seems to be, "If I'm not there, I'm not alcoholic."

The leader's first reaction to a member's absence should be to ask why. The position this group leader takes is that there are only two acceptable reasons: death and serious or contagious illness. And although he announces this in a facetious way at the first session, the underlying tone is one of seriousness.

Absences can be motivated by a lack of commitment or interest. Sometimes they are motivated by fear—of the group (so *many* people to talk to!), or of the changes the member might have to make (Johnson, 1963). Sometimes the absences are a response to shyness and embarrassment. It should be remembered that many alcoholics never learned how to relate to other people because the interpersonal style that they developed was characterized by distance between themselves and others. But whatever the reasons for the absence, they are irrelevant because they are destructive to the group. Alcoholics know this, which is why they are very sensitive to a member's absence. Absentees are conspicuous. They are prime topics of conversation and create far more hostility among group members than concern. Why? The answer is that whatever the particular motive for the absence, somewhere in it is an element of rejection of the group. Alcoholics focus on that. From their viewpoint they are, after much conflict and vacillation, reaching out to a group of people for support—and one of them does not show up? They find it infuriating.

What the leader should be aware of in such a case is that the members' discussion of the absentee should not be allowed to serve as a way of avoiding other personal concerns. While members are expressing their feelings, they should be led to understand that it is important for them to develop constructive methods for dealing with the absentee, since they, not the leader, should assume this task. The message to the absentee should focus on obligation and responsibility. At the same time, the absentee should learn that he or she was missed and that there was concern about the absence. Absences are not going to occur as often when the group is able to create a positive climate, one that is, in addition to all else, forgiving.

Silence

Silent members in group often are members who at best are struggling with the denial defense. They are not absolutely sure yet whether they have come to accept the fact of their addiction—ergo their silence.

In an earlier work dealing with the alcoholic client, the author pointed out (Perez, 1985) that silence in individual counseling can be attributed to: (1) embarrassment; (2) resentment, hostility, and anger; (3) testing of the counselor; (4) conflict; (5) fear; or (6) the need to integrate what has been said. These reasons are applicable to the group as well.

Silence in group seems to generate even more anxiety than it does in individual counseling. It seems that the degree of anxiety is in direct proportion to the number of members—the more members there are, the more tension and anxiety are aroused.

In one of the earliest treatments of the topic, Hinckley and Herman (1951) interpreted silence in the group to mean: (1) members were punishing the leader; (2)members were trying to avoid the reality of the moment; (3) members were using the silence as a veil to hide behind; or (4) there was a problem in communication. These explanations have as much validity today as when the authors disclosed them.

Silences occur in the most dynamic and alive groups and for all the reasons mentioned. A new counselor usually finds them especially anxiety provoking because they are interpreted as a manifestation of the counselor's ineptness.

How, then, can silence be handled?

1. The leader can sit, wait, and let the tension build. By doing so the leader communicates that the group is in charge of its climate and its hour and can do with both as it pleases.
2. The leader can initiate a favorite group activity.
3. The leader can break the silence by commenting on any personal feelings about it.
4. The leader can interpret the meaning of the silence, that is, that it seems to take place immediately after someone has cracked a joke, become angry, etc.
5. The leader may question selected members as to why they think the silence occurs. Members whom the leader is confident would welcome the question would be chosen.

Antagonism

Antagonistic members are those who still deny their alcoholism in some measure. More often than not, their denial is supported by projection. They are very suspicious of others. Both defenses are invariably complemented by fantasy. Antagonistic members are prone to create images in which they picture themselves as being victimized or, paradoxically, as being destructive. Such images both justify and generate their antagonism.

Antagonistic members inspire destructive anxiety and tension in the group. Antagonism is an integral part of the alcoholic personality. It shows itself at group meetings too frequently, if not directly in words between members, then certainly in the tone with which a comment is made. The humor among alcoholics is seldom nondirected and ironic. More often it is personal, sarcastic, and demeaning.

The specific reasons for this vary from group to group but underlying these specifics are certain commonalities.

1. Testing. The logic among members goes like this. How much needling you take from me shows how much you really accept me and how much I can really trust you. This testing aspect is evidenced in the fact that verbal brutalizing among the members is found most frequently and is the most vitriolic in the initial sessions. As the members get to know each other (and pass each other's tests!), there is a significant decline in verbal abuse.

2. Social ineptness. Not uncommonly the male alcoholic who constantly displays an antagonism toward others is beset with a deep sense of machismo. Deep down in this person's perception of others is the warped idea that to show courtesy and kindness, especially to a male peer, is not masculine. Such a person tends to view kindness and gentleness as feminine traits, and for that reason may actually fear them. This type of male alcoholic adheres to such actions in general because he simply never learned how to relate with respect and gentleness.

3. Fear, and its constant associate, suspicion. These are also common factors in the antagonism of the alcoholic new to a group. If one stranger is a threat, consider how much of a threat five to a dozen are!

The best antidote for the antagonistic member is warmth, trust, and candor. It is not confrontation. Confrontation only fuels antagonism; it feeds into the member's initial perception. The leader who promotes a climate of unconditioned positive regard for the group and communicates that every member is entitled to share in it will go a long way toward mitigating member antagonism.

In most groups there are members who have their antagonism under control. These members can easily engage in warm, accepting, trusting interaction. Leaders should support and promote such interactions.

The experienced group leader of alcoholics understands that it took the antagonistic members a long time to develop their antagonism and that they have been living with it even longer. The fact is that the antagonism is not going to go away quickly and easily. What is also true is that more often than not the understanding and the patience group leaders show with antagonistic members will be emulated and generalized by other group members. In such a climate, antagonism inevitably decreases.

Manipulating

Manipulating members incorporate most of the defenses of antagonistic members. Like the latter they have not given up on the fact that they might not be alcoholic. Also like the antagonistic member, they suspect other's motives and fantasize about being victimized. The essential difference between the two is that manipulators are not usually blunt, direct, or violent.

Manipulation is the inevitable and constant response to feeling restricted. Manipulators, to justify their manipulation, learn to perceive a controlling world, and ironically one filled with manipulators. This is, of course, a common alcoholic view of the world and the people in it. This alcoholic view, the obsession about being manipulated, was once colorfully expressed in group like this. "It's all a big game, boy, all a big game. Everybody wants something. Even the do-gooders and the bleeding hearts. They want something. They want to make you over into their image. If you don't know, boy, I'll tell you. Everybody's got their little bag. Everybody's got something to sell. And they all want you to buy it." The alcoholic response is, of course, not only *not* to buy "it" (their rehabilitation) but far more, to manipulate everybody (themselves included) into believing that they are not alcoholic.

Manipulators can operate from a position of weakness as well as a position of strength. Utilizing the Gestalt concepts of underdog and top dog, Shastrom (1967) has pointed out the considerable variety of manipulator types and their most common respective behaviors.

Manipulator	*Behavior*
	From a position of weakness (underdog)
Weakling	Sensitive to hurt
Clinging vine	Dependent
Nice guy	Warm
	From a position of strength (top dog)
The judge	Critical
The bully	Aggressive
The calculator	Controlling
The dictator	Strong
The protector	Supportive

In dealing with alcoholic manipulators, the leader needs to bear in mind that with respect to blaming they are externally, not internally, oriented. Their problems, they are convinced, stem from the outside, not the inside. Simply put, people are their problems, not themselves. It is other people who have a bag of something they are trying to sell, not they. On entry into the group, they tend to perceive the leader and other group members as precisely these other people.

Simple explanations by the leaders can ameliorate the view that the manipulator holds of them. They can do this by explaining their role and the members' roles (see Chapter IV on administrative functions). Complementing these explanations should be discussions and activities that focus on self-examination.

Finally, manipulation in alcoholic group interplay is inevitable. Effective group leaders themselves are manipulators of necessity. An important point to note, however, is that leader manipulations are directed toward helping all of the group members perceive that people can indeed be enhancing as well as destructive.

Housekeeping

Often the alcoholic group is saddled with a member who has a strong inclination toward physical activity. Such a member cheerfully moves chairs around as needed, sets up the ashtrays (empties them during the session), not uncommonly cooks and brings in food (everything from cookies to lasagna), and generally looks after the group. In session this person is constantly bouncing around, nodding, smiling, serving, is in constant motion. The group generally looks upon such a person as a character and almost always as likeable. This type of person has been termed the housekeeper.

Housekeepers might be pleasant but, like the preceding four types, continue to deny their alcoholism. They are also fantasizers. Housekeepers tend to set themselves up in their own little worlds as protectors of others. Complementing both denial and fantasy are elaborate rationalizations to justify their basic need; that is not to face their alcoholism and/or the problems that led to it.

With physical activity housekeepers are able to meet their manifest and too obvious objective—to be a part of the group. At the same time, their frantic activity provides them with the opportunity to meet their unconscious and more important object; namely, *not* to involve themselves emotionally in the group and thereby not confront their own problems.

Group members with effective guidance can help the housekeeper. They can do so by combining praise for what the housekeeper has done with encouragement to let others also give to the group. The combination of reward and encouragement to share seems to foster self-disclosure and more personal involvement by the pure housekeeper type.

Some housekeeper types' problems and behavior are componded by the need to "parent." The parenting need seems to be motivated by the need for power over the group. (The more power particular members have, the less they need to deal with their own addiction.) Thus the parent serves as another member's protector. "Parent" types usually anticipate the leader's move to protect abused members. They are so good at this anticipation that they invariably have a debilitating effect on one or more of the members by making such members dependent upon them.

In short, in both zeal and competence they are able to meet peer members' needs. They find much "heady" reward in their ability to nurture. Their problem and their destructiveness are comparable to those of the overprotective parent—*they cannot let go* because their need is not to meet member or group needs but their own.

If the behavior of parent-housekeeper types is not interrupted, and soon, it bodes poorly for group progress. The reason for this is that once parent-housekeepers feel that they control even one member, they may seek to function as surrogate leaders (and they will not have to deal with their own alcoholism at all).

Most parent-type housekeepers seem to be oblivious to the destructive effects of their behavior on their dependent member and on the group. The best leader approach to this type is confrontation. The objective is to point out that overprotectiveness is just another form of the enabling that precipitates alcoholism.

Clowning

Sometimes the group includes a clown, a person who makes everybody laugh whenever possible with a joke or a witticism, both of which serve to hide the denial defense.

The clown's emotional rationale can be stated as a question: "How can I possibly be an incapacitated alcoholic if I make people laugh?" Within this rationale there is a lot of rationalization.

The clown's humor, unlike that of the antagonist, usually is not hostile and anxiety provoking but is funny and relieves tension. Everybody likes the clown because the clown is an entertainer and everybody likes to be entertained. When the clown feels in top form the stage is set for the possibility of a whole comic routine. When in such a mood, everybody seems to have a good time. The point, of course, is that an alcoholic group does not assemble to be entertained. Continued and protracted clowning in the alcoholic group should be seen precisely for what it is—a very sophisticated form of resistance. Moreover, it can take the focus and attention away from, or at least underplay, the seriousness of the members' problems.

The clown who is an alcoholic is a fascinating paradox. Alcoholics ordinarily are not emotionally invested in others. Alcoholics generally are alcoholic because they are invested primarily in themselves. This is not true of the clown. The clown clowns to make people laugh. And the laughter obtained reaps rewards, since clowns are usually the center of attention.

The veneer of "clown" is usually a thick one and very difficult to penetrate. This is especially true with the alcoholic because such a veneer suits the alcoholic's purpose exceedingly well—to be alone. The leader must be aware, then, that once a group member has become established as the clown, it is very difficult to deal with that person. The recommendation here is not to let it happen. Once clowns have elicited any measurable laughter, they want more. Their need for it is insatiable. Moreover, once one has become established as a kind of court jester, it is difficult for members to alter their perceptions. One cannot take a clown seriously because the usual view is that clowns have no problems. Consciously or unconsciously, alcoholic clowns work very hard at establishing and maintaining that perception of themselves.

How should leaders deal with clowns? The focus should be on the motives behind the clowns' humor. In group one motive certainly is to camouflage their own problems and direct attention to someone else. Accordingly leaders must constantly bear in mind that the clown is there for the same reason as everyone else and that point must be communicated to the whole group. While it is alright to laugh with them, it is far more beneficial for the clown types, and the group, if leaders respond seriously to them and to what underlies their humor.

Professionalizing

An interesting phenomenon in counseling the alcoholic group is the increasing number of professional members whom one meets. These are the people who have been members of prior groups (alcoholic and others).

Professional members continue to be professional members because they deny their alcoholism. The denial is often supported by a smooth, sophisticated intellectualization defense. Professional members like to think they are convincing speakers. This is probably so because woven into their defense structures are little fantasies about being powerful and in control.

Their behavior is frequently both personally resistant and destructive. From the initial session, they seem to want to project an image of a "senior member" or even of a cocounselor. (Dinkmeyer & Muro, 1971). Thus they will use psychological or counseling lingo, which they sprinkle with such terms as transference, dynamics, and rapport. If other members are not duly impressed, professional members may move on and try using leadership techniques, including interpreting and questioning. Other members invariably find their approach irritating and condescending. Occasionally at a very early session, professional members will seem to share and self-disclose. Typically the disclosure turns out to be material that they discussed in a previous group.

Professional members love to advise. Powdermaker and Frank (1953) have pointed out that advice giving in group is a way of drawing attention away from one's own problems, and may be a way of hiding feelings of contempt for the one to whom it is given. At the same time, some professional members are good at giving advice. They intersperse it with illustrations and an affable humor, and seem to be supportive of the group. They then may work themselves into the role of "Delphic oracle." If they are successful in such a role, group members may look to them for alternative courses of action, or before embarking on specific ventures, whether vocational, social, or even therapeutic. Ensconced in such a role, the one they were seeking all along, professional members are able to meet the two needs that are so important to them—to obtain status in the group's eyes and to avoid confrontation of their own problems by themselves or others.

Given free rein such members would pose a real challenge to the leader's role and would be a devisive force in the group process. The best way to deal with them is to prevent the problem from occurring in the first place. Prudent leaders, when forming a group, will try to place at least two experienced members in the group. More often than not, they check each other out. If they do not, the leader can ally with the weaker of the two to maintain group cohesion. Frequently all that is needed is a private meeting with the member to point out the objectives of the group and what the member's real role is.

The leader might try using the group to confront professional members. But this can be risky because it has to be done at the initial sessions, when members do not know each other very well. A professional member may be just as vulnerable as any other member. Finally, it must be remembered that professional members are still in treatment because prior experience was not beneficial or was not enough. In their own way, they are still trying to achieve and/or maintain sobriety. The point is that too harsh or too early confrontation of professional members by the group might hurt more than help not only the professional, but the group as well.

ENHANCING BEHAVIORS

EHANCING BEHAVIORS are those that the leader and members utilize to facilitate the process and progress of the group. Ordinarily it is the leader who first uses these behaviors. If the leader is an effective model and the members follow, their destructive perception, characterized primarily by the defense of denial, begins to alter to sublimation and the group moves steadily toward health and sobriety.

The responsibility to be enhancing, however, is not solely the leader's. The alcoholic members share in this responsibility as it is their health that is the focus and the issue of concern. The group's motivation to effect these behaviors and thereby enhance each other is inexorably tied up with the individual members' particular desire to achieve and maintain sobriety.

The enhancing behaviors are:

1. Self-disclosing.
2. Trusting.
3. Facilitating.
4. Giving feedback.
5. Listening.
6. Communicating.

Self-disclosing

Freud first observed that people seemed to improve emotionally if they talked about their problems when he was working with Joseph Breuer, before he even went into the practice of dealing with the "nervous disorders." The improvement was especially marked if participants shared and confided their most hidden and private concerns. Today we call this "self-disclosing" and it is critical to recovery in alcoholism counseling.

When members begin to self-disclose, it is significant because it means that their denial defense is beginning to abate. In addition, it means that they are beginning to perceive more optimistically. These components are necessary if members are going to invest emotionally in the group.

For self-disclosure to take place, the climate has to be the one touted as the most favorable by Rogerian counselors—one of warmth, trust, and unconditional positive regard. But again, the process and responsibility for achieving this atmosphere lie with the alcoholics.

The most positive aspect of self-disclosing is that it invariably promotes trust and brings about closeness in the group. Self-disclosing meets one of the most stringent criterion for effective process in the alcoholic group: that the atmosphere be one of candor and authenticity. It is impossible to self-disclose honestly and retain a veneer of pretension. Its unique value for the alcoholic group is that it militates against paranoia.

Trusting

The trusting member is one in whom denial has been, or is being, replaced by the sublimation defense. Such a member, consciously or unconsciously, has decided that the road to health lies in putting faith in others.

One's capacity to trust is very much related to one's capacity to love. Thus when people love, they trust that their emotional investment in the other person will not be violated. Trust promotes feelings of self-worth in the person trusted and in the person doing the trusting.

Group members are obliged to maintain confidentiality regarding all that is said and transpires in a session. Without this confidentiality the group process is impossible. Poppen and Thompson (1974) have pointed out that the ability to maintain confidentialities is a function of trust. It is only when group members trust that they will self-disclose. Once a foundation of trust has been established, members can risk exposing themselves.

Trust does not come easily to alcoholics. Their history invaribly includes having the love and trust that they invested in others violated.

Leaders need first to make clear that they recognize the difficulties involved in trusting. At the same time, they need to stress that the group can function only if each member respects group confidentiality. And confidentiality, it should be pointed out, is based on trust.

In explaining this issue of trust and confidentiality to the group, the author likes to use the analogy that each member is a link in the group chain. Any members who have disclosed another member's confidence will have broken the chain and effectively broken up the group. Thus each member must be made to realize that the group's integrity and life hinge on each member's sense of personal responsibility and trustworthiness.

Facilitating

Facilitating in group is simply the manifestation of the sublimation defense. Facilitators do all the things that should be done in the group. At the first session, the leader is usually the sole facilitator, though sometimes the group is lucky enough to include a member who, by both disposition and temperament, is inclined to participate more as a facilitator than as a member in need.

What do facilitators do? They get members involved. Their looks, smiles, and tone promote closeness among members. This is no small feat in a group of alcoholics who do not know one another. Facilitators are generally concerned with meeting the needs of all the members. They find personal reward in doing so and are effective with alcoholics because they are able to communicate that fact. The effect of that communicating is to accelerate group progress.

The emotional antennae of the facilitators are fine-tuned to all the members of the group. They are sensitive and respond appropriately to the emotions of group members indicated by nuances in tone, expression, and body stances.

The alcoholics who function as facilitators can best be understood as alcoholics in accelerated recovery. Such people have, for whatever reasons, retained the best of their internal aloneness orientation and have learned to integrate it with a newly found external orientation.

Facilitators beget facilitators. Effective leader facilitators will invariably find members who want to and can identify with them. In the alcoholic group, member facilitators seem to be even better facilitators than the leader as their peers seem to identify with them more easily than they do with the leader.

The best effect of member facilitation seems to be an increase in group self-esteem and responsibility. With both of these, there is, appropriately enough, a corresponding decline in leader activity.

Giving Feedback*

When the leader or alcoholic members tell a given member how they feel about the latter's behavior, it is called giving feedback. It is an indispensable requisite to group progress. It is the way members are helped. Through feedback alcoholics learn what many have never learned, what is and what is not appropriate.

The beauty of feedback is that it is remarkably democratic. When one gives feedback, it is always in terms of one's own perception of reality. Thus the person who does it prefaces any observation with: "My feeling is . . ." or "What I'm hearing is . . ." or "I can't speak for anybody else but my impression is. . . ." There are no absolutes when one gives feedback. It is always in terms of one's own subjective perception. For this reason the probability and risk of threat to the recipients of the feedback (so vitally important with alcoholics) are minimized. In such a situation the recipients are encouraged to accept or reject various aspects of both feedback and their own behavior.

Listening

When writing about the teaching process, Moustakas (1966) observed that "when we are listened to, it creates us, makes us unfold and expand" (p. 42). The observation is especially appropriate for group counseling. The conviction here is that a group in which listening to others is stressed is a group in which the members will "unfold and expand."

Alcoholics are often charged with the fact that they never listen. It is probably true. However, it must be realized that they probably never learned how because they felt that no one ever listened to them.

This problem that alcoholics have with listening to others and being listened to can be rectified in group. Once members learn to listen to each other, they find that their anger and their need to play games decrease rapidly.

In the alcoholic group, especially initially, effective listening is dif-

*In this behavior, and in listening and communicating (which follow), the prime defense is sublimation.

ficult. The obstacle of not having ever learned to listen is compounded by the fact that the group climate is usually an emotionally charged one. In such a climate, members can and do speak with anger, offer unwanted advice to each other, and often interrupt with irrelevant questions. To promote an atmosphere of listening, the leader will need to deal with each of these destructive behaviors. The leader's most constructive approach, however, will be by example. (See "The Group: Stages and Techniques" Chapter VI.) Activities for group members to learn listening skills are outlined in Chapter VII.

Communicating

Those members communicate who speak, *to* and not *about* each other. The leader can effect this quickly at the first session by asking members to address each other, by pointing out to them that group communication is not filtered through the leader and that the only messages the leader needs to get are those directed to the leader personally.

Both the Rogerian and the Gestalt rationales outlined in Chapter I take the view that members communicate when their words, emotions, and behavior come together. Members who communicate, then, are not only in touch with their feelings, but with their bodies as well. Trotzer (1977) terms this type of cummunication "leveling," which he describes as the "open expression of members as they really are and feel" (p. 161).

Whatever the view or the orientation, the reality is that communication between and among members is a function of all the enhancing behaviors described; that is, self-disclosing, trusting, and so forth.

For the alcoholic there is no more important lesson to be learned in group than that of communication. The one who learns it progresses, reinforces the maintenance of sobriety. The one who does not learn communication is in trouble. Alcoholics who do not communicate continue to live in lonely worlds. And these lonely worlds are filled with all the elements that fuel alcoholism—suspicion, hostility, and a sense of victimization.

The leader who is able to help members feel secure about their position in group will promote communication. The more secure alcoholic members feel about their position in relation to their peers, the better they communicate. This security helps them to speak directly without offending or embarrassing others. As they are able to do this more and more, their sense of security within the group increases, and more important, their sense of internal security becomes greater. The benefits to the group are incalcuable as their communicative abilities seem to become generalized among the other members. This is predictable and the reason for it is not difficult to fathom. Quite simply, everybody wants to communicate—especially alcoholics.

EXTREME BEHAVIORS

In the third category of behaviors are those termed extreme. These are the most difficult to deal with. Some embarrass both leader and members. All of them can be threatening because they emanate exclusively from an emotional base. When members behave in an extreme way, they are telling the group that they have lost all cognitive and mental control.

Extreme behaviors, by definition, are those found at opposite ends of the emotional continuum. Thus a person may operate like an acutely dependent baby and weep throughout a session, or may intimidate, act in rage, and effectively force a group into submission.

Extreme behavior is often a function of conflict. Alcoholics who are in the grips of a BUD conflict—they want to drink but are inhibited from doing so by conscience—are prime candidates for extreme acting out. Members who are under a "buzz" often are the ones who affect extreme talk and behavior. Alcohol lowers defenses, clouds ego judgment, and increases the probability of engaging in primitive behavior.

Extreme behavior by one member can trigger it in another, whether it be crying, rage, or affection. The reality is that group sessions can be intensely emotional. To be effective leaders must understand the source and nature of extreme behavior. Armed with this understanding, they can be ready with ideas and strategies to help the group cope.

There are any number of affective extremes. The dynamics and methods of treatment considered here should equip leaders with the basic rationale to deal with others. Three extreme behaviors found in the alcoholic group are weeping, assaulting, and seducing.

Weeping

Children cry to obtain nurturance—so do alcoholics in group. For this reason weeping is generally interpreted as a function of the regression defense.

No emotion can create a feeling of embarrassment among a group of alcoholics, male or female, faster than weeping. At the same time, especially when women are in the group, it is the most common of the extreme affective behaviors. Most male members do not seem to become inured to it, or even used to it.

Men in this culture know that they are not supposed to weep. Weeping for most men is associated with softness and femininity. Women can have "a good cry" if life gets hard, but a *man* cannot. Unfortuntely alcoholic men are as addicted to this distorted machismo-like thnking about tears as they are to alcohol. It is probably the reason they seldom cry. That is regrettable because although men who cry might suffer acute embarrassment, the experience can have a very positive effect upon them, and ultimately upon the group, too. The author's experience has been that men who, prior to crying, were antagonistic, indifferent, withdrawn, and clownish, afterward tend to be more involved, more tolerant, more accepting, and much more interested in the group. At the same time, men who "break down and cry" (even our expressions condemn the act) may not return. This counselor has seen that, too. It is probably this fear of breakdown and the consequent threat of feeling compelled to drop out of the group that precipitates an occasional male member's mumbled request to be excused to go to the toilet.

Nevertheless at times alcoholic group counseling can be heart-rending and it is for this reason that groups develop systems to mitigate the embarrassment of having cried. What this counselor has observed (about himself, too) is that when a member is sharing a particularly painful experience, and people are furtively wiping their eyes, no one looks at anyone.

To deal effectively with weeping, counselors need to know what their own feelings are about it. If they are embarrassed by it, they will communicate that to the group. If they are casual, tolerant, and accepting of it, they will communicate that, too. Counselors who hold to the latter position should understand that what they need to communicate to the members is that they fully appreciate how difficult it is to cry, that attitudes about it are personal. The position here is that weeping finally is just another way for humans to express their pain and frustration. Once it has taken place, the weeping can facilitate a member's progress.

Assaulting

Projection is the common supporting defense for the assaultive alcoholic's displacement defense. These alcoholics live with a lot of suspicions that they constantly attribute to others.

Leaders who are able to help the alcoholic group create a warm, nonjudgmental climate of trust often find that in such a climate members may feel comfortable enough to ventilate, to displace upon peers and upon themselves. As has been noted, sex and age notwithstanding, a common denominator in the personalities of alcoholics is antagonism. Alcoholism and antagonism are first cousins. How antagonism is displayed in the particular individual depends on the intensity of the feeling and on the person's controls.

When the alcoholic is verbally oriented and is reasonably well controlled, the problem can be dealt with without much difficulty. If the member verbally displaces the anger upon another member, the leader can, if necessary, step in to protect and defend. Such activity is almost routine in the alcoholic group.

It is when the alcoholic is not verbally but is physically oriented and is seething with hostility that there may be problems. If this person's control mechanisms are weak, problems are virtually guaranteed. The worry in these cases is the potential for physical assault.

The competent group counselor quickly learns whether there are any in the group who may be assaultive. Should the counselor even suspect that there are, it is prudent to have the group immediately establish a very clear rule against physical aggression of any kind, with the bottom line being expulsion from the group.

Rules, however, are only rules, and the "meant to be broken" rationalization is a way of life for many alcoholics. Certainly there is little guarantee that one who has learned to resort to assault would be restrained by such a rule however firm and clear it might be. Nevertheless, not to establish such a rule might be interpreted as a green light to assault.

Expulsion may be necessary at times. At the same time, it must be recognized that physically aggressive behavior is the prime way, and sometimes the only way, that some alcoholics (especially males), know to release anger and frustration. Is it the responsibility of an alcoholism group to help a member learn other ways? The answer to this question lies with both leader and group. A group may be composed of one or more members whose family life was characterized by physical abuse. For some members, being assaulted, or even seeing it in the group, resurrects all the horror they have been trying to escape. Such experiences are traumatic. They do not need them, and certainly not in a setting designed to be therapeutic.

When the group contains such members, it may be appropriate to drop the member who has been assaultive or to consider transfer. This can be done in group or by the leader in private, whichever is more appropriate for both member and group.

It also should be noted that there are many self-referred, recovering alcoholics who strive hard, if not heroically, to overcome their physical acting out. There are groups that can handle such people and do it effectively. The author remembers vividly a case involving Martha, a woman in her early 40s who angered easily and responded stridently. The author never thought she would become assaultive because she was articulate and expressed herself freely and easily. Such ventilation, it was thought, would take care of her deep-seated antagonisms. In an intense moment, while she literally was ranting, a man who was still playing clown punctuated one of her sentences with an ironic quip. She turned and slapped him, first on his left cheek with her palm, then on the right with the back of her hand. The group was stunned and fell into an embarrassed silence. The woman sat down and began to weep quietly.

The group handled the situation well. It was the clown who observed, "Well, I deserved that." And the woman replied, "No one deserves that." She then proceeded to share with the group the classic tale of the alcoholic child. Martha had been physically abused by both alcoholic parents and had begun to do the same with her children. It was not the leader but the one who had been slapped who observed, "I think you want help, Martha. That's why you slapped me. You knew I'd take it better than anybody else here." She agreed that she wanted help. the group agreed to help. Four years later Martha continues straight down recovery road without making a single detour while the clown has made a dozen or more.

There are, of course, activities that can be employed to deal with those whom a leader feels are potentially assaultive. The idea behind such activities is that they reduce tension and the impulse to act out physically. Members who concur in their potential to be violent could, on group request, do push-ups, or hit a punching ball or a pillow. Arm wrestling with several members in succession is also good therapy. A very effective technique is the "time out." According to prearranged agreement with the potentially assaultive person, members can call time out. The person then chooses a neutral member from the group to confer with alone until the neutral member feels the person can return to group. Finally, the group can establish a policy whereby members who feel they can become violent can ask to isolate themselves for short periods.

Seducing

As used here seducing means effectively to blend one's verbal and emotional competencies with body (if need be) to obtain from others whatever one wants. Seducing can be motivated by the desire for money, for sex, to make a favorable impression, to alter a point of view. The experience of alcohol addiction provides for many a kind of perverted schooling for becoming an effective seducer. The curriculum demands that one learn to mask aggressiveness with a mixture of dependency and nurturance and to set forth a credible image of candor and honesty.

Seducing alcoholics fantasize a lot. If men, the focus of their fantasies is on power and controlling others. If women, they live in worlds where their requests are viewed as commands, instantly obeyed. Both are effective seducers in their fantasy worlds. The problems occur when they try to translate their fantasies into reality.

As would be expected, alcoholics are acutely sensitive to the seducing group participant. If their needs are confused or strong enough, however, they can also be remarkably vulnerable to such a member. Not long ago Jack, a handsome young man in his early 30s, joined a group of mine which no one had joined, nor from which anybody had been terminated, for approximately six weeks. The group climate to that point had been warm and enhancing. The housekeeping member was named

Betty. She was in her early 40s, heavy-set and brown-haired. She continued to bring in cookies with everybody's approval, but her need to nurture and control had abated as her motivation to self-disclose increased. The only other woman in the group was Alice. She was blonde, slender, and pretty. Her initial shyness had declined to a great extent and she had begun to participate more and more. At the last two meetings, Alice, with Betty's strong encouragement and the group's approval, had brought in chocolate cakes.

At the first meeting, Jack was quiet. Nobody pressed him. At the second session, however, he began to interact generally and easily, and quite apparently made a very strong and positive impression on the men as well as the women.

It was at the very next session that changes began to take place. Jack made some quiet, appropriate comments to Betty about her cookies and ate two pieces of Alice's cake. His glances at Alice were even more flattering than his comments. Despite Jack's positive comments to both women, I felt a strange, uncommon tension in the air. Group members, I thought, were speaking more sharply. Betty was wearing cosmetics for the first time and received compliments from most of the men, but not from Alice. In turn, she did not compliment Alice on her cake, nor did she ask her to bring one for the following session.

At the next session, Betty came in with a new hair style. Alice showed up in clothes that were markedly tighter than usual. The group's interactions were now characterized by protracted silences. All the men had become quieter. It seemed as though some of them were feeling more like observers than participants. Interactions that had been casual, facile, and meaningful were now anxious and banal.

I wondered if Jack was aware of the effect he was creating. I began to ask questions focused on the group climate. How was it now? How comfortable were we now? What changes had occurred in the past several weeks. Why? I asked these questions of no one in particular. They were the questions, however, that everybody, including the women, had been waiting for. The responses and the discussion that followed inevitably led to Jack.

The ventilation upon him at one point became so vitriolic that Betty called him a cheap womanizer! I intervened and pointed out that the group in general was to some degree responsible, that most of the men had meekly surrendered both their roles and positions in the group. I pointed out, too, that while Betty and Alice had not sought to be seduced, they had at least rewarded Jack's efforts by their talk, dress, and behavior toward one another.

Initially surprised, even shocked by the group's reaction, Jack became very withdrawn and at the end of the session privately asked me to be transferred to another group. (He was on a court-mandated referral for drunken driving.) I pointed out that his way of relating had probably contributed to his alcoholism and had become an integral part of his makeup. I told him that the group could help if he wanted it to. At the end of each of the next two sessions, at which he maintained his withdrawn position, he again asked to be transferred. I agreed for two reasons. Jack's nonparticiption was causing much discomfort in the group, and he obviously was not ready to change.

SUMMARY

DESTRUCTIVE BEHAVIORS can be understood as a function of resistance. Common forms of destructive behaviors in the alcoholic group are absence, silence, antagonizing, manipulating, housekeeping, clowning, and professionalizing. The leader should be aware that these behaviors can be especially insidious when they go underground, as they do with the more sophisticated participants.

Enhancing behaviors are those that facilitate the process and progress of the group. Ordinarily leaders display these behaviors in the initial stages of the group. The responsibility to be enhancing is not solely that of the leader, however. Members share in it, too. The enhancing behaviors discussed were self-disclosing, trusting, facilitating, giving feedback, listening, and communicating.

The most difficult behaviors to deal with are the extreme behaviors. Some embarrass the group, all of them threaten. Extreme behaviors tend to be at opposite ends of the emotional continuum. Extreme behavior by one member can trigger it in another, whether it be crying, rage, or affection. The extreme behaviors discussed were weeping, assaulting, and seducing.

REFERENCES

Becker, B. J. The psychodynamics of analytic group psychotherapy. *Am J Psychoanal* 32:177–185, 1972.

Dinkmeyer, D. C., and Muro, J. D. *Group Counseling: Therapy and Practice* Itascu, Ill.: Peacock, 1971.

Hinckley, R. G., and Herman, L. *Group Treatmention Psychotherapy.* Minneapolis: University of Minnesota Press, 1951.

Johnson, J. A. *Group Therapy: A Practical Approach.* New York: McGraw-Hill, 1963.

Moustakas, C. E. *The Authentic Teacher.* Cambridge, Mass.: Howard A. Doyle Publishing Co., 1966, p. 42.

Perez, J. F. *Counseling the Alcoholic.* Muncie, Ind.: Accelerated Development, 1985.

Poppen, W. A., and Thompson C. L. *School Counseling: Theories and Concepts.* Lincoln, Neb.: Professional Educators Publications, 1974.

Powdermaker, F. B., and Frank, J. D. *Group Psychotherapy.* Cambridge, Mass.: Harvard University Press, 1953.

Shastrom, E. L. *Man the Manipulator: The Inner Journey from Manipulation to Actualization.* New York: Abingdon Press, 1967.

Trotzer, J. P. *The Counselor and the Group: Integrating Theory, Training and Practice.* Monterey, Calif.: Brooks/Cole, 1977, p.161.

Chapter IV

The Group Counselor

COUNSELOR PERCEPTION

General Research

As was noted in Chapter II, how group clients perceive others will determine how well or how poorly they relate to the group. This is true for the counselor, too. The research evidence is that counselors perceive their clients optimistically. The counselor view is "therapeutic" and basically "positive" (Hart, 1975–76). Predictably, the effects of such perception are desirable. Leake and King (1977) found that those counselors who were the most successful with their skid-row alcoholics had an optimistic view about their recovery. They were able to communicate to their clients that they expected them to achieve and maintain a status of recovery. In a study with a comparable alcoholic population (Bowery alcoholics), Talbot and Gillen (1978) found that the critical determinant for a therapeutic outcome was not so much the counselor's professional background and training but rather the perceptions held by the counselor.

How counselors perceive their clients will, in turn, influence how clients perceive them. Rutan and Rice (1981) found that group members perceive their leaders as more than human, even as having charismatic powers. Wile (1976) found that clients' perceptions were determined by the personal qualities exhibited by the counselors. Scheid (1976) found that the counselor's personal qualities influenced client perception of the counselor's competence, the therapaeutic climate, and client satisfaction. All these findings were corroborated in a study by Valle (1981). This research showed that the clients of counselors who are especially empathic and genuine are less likely to lapse back into drinking and less likely to use any alcohol for the first two years after counseling.

Another important factor in how effectively counselors function with their clients has to do with their professional ethics and values. It was just such a view that led Hertzman and Mitnick (1978–79) to recommend that curriculum units dealing with values and ethics be included in any training program for alcoholism counselors. Implicit in this recommendation is the idea that in working with alcoholics counselors are constantly making value judgments. These affect not only the therapeutic progress of the clients but their whole lives.

One of the most all-inclusive studies dealing with counselor values was that done by Menne (1975), who had 75 practicing counselors give their opinions as to what values counselors need to hold if they are to be effective. These opinions were then edited and organized into a research instrument of 132 "competencies." With this instrument Menne surveyed 376 counselors. When their responses were rank ordered, the top three were:

1. Professional ethics. How the counselor acts in relation to clients was given top rating. It was felt that counselors should have a definitive understanding of their own ethics.
2. Self-awareness. Counselors felt that a knowledge of self was a critical factor in functioning effectively. Key aspects of the self-knowledge involved a full appreciation of what their attitudes, values, and biases were.
3. Personal characteristics. These had to do particularly with interpersonal sensitivity, maturity, and flexibility, both in and out of counseling.

What such findings reveal is that counselors believe that to be effective with clients they must have a clear, personal rationale. They have to know where they are coming from and where they are going. Clarity about both is the prerequisite to counselor success.

Author's Findings

In an earlier publication, this author reported on research with six counselors of families and other groups (Perez, 1979). These counselors perceived their effectiveness as being based upon:

1. A need to help others. Their belief was that counselors who can find reward in giving will themselves reap rich rewards.
2. A willingness to take risks in the counseling process "in order to effect healthful changes." Such a willingness, they believed, was rooted in the counselor's emotional security.
3. Flexibility. They perceived the effective counselor as one who could "shift gears emotionally."

In a subsequent investigation (Perez, 1985) with experienced counselors of alcoholics, this author found the following.

1. Counselors perceive optimistically and build their relationship on this optimism. To be successful with alcoholics, counselors have to adhere to the belief that they will achieve sobriety.
2. Counselors perceive realistically. The alcoholic, they reported, is a person "who is in a great deal of pain—whose thinking is distorted." What these counselors communicated is that the effective counselor can be both optimistic and realistic about the alcoholic client.
3. Counselors perceive empathically. An effective alcoholism counselor is one who is not only willing to perceive the world that the client perceives, but is able to communicate that willingness. Counselor empathy, they believe, is a critical ingredient in the effective counseling of the alcoholic.

Selected Counselors' Perceptions

It is important to report the research on counselor perception as it provides data that are both intellectualized and objective. At the same time, perception, like the group counseling process itself, is quite the opposite; it is emotional and subjective. Simply stated, perception is very personalized. It was precisely to inject a personalized touch that the author asked three practicing alcoholism counselors to share their perceptions of what qualities make an effective group counselor.

1. *Male, 27 years old, five years' experience as a group counselor.*

"I see the qualities that make for an effective counselor as being part and parcel of all the therapeutic functions. The most important function I have as a group counselor of alcoholics is that of being an effective role model. In that capacity all my personal and professional qualities are on display. Being an effective role model is fundamental for intervention and promotion of health. Experience has taught me that newly recovering alcoholics are very suspicious of anything that is not genuine. If I am not healthy and comfortable with who I am, they will not listen to or respect the ground rules that I set forth for the group. In other words the newly recovering alcoholics are so suspicious and reluctant to share honestly anything they feel that they will not share until they have thoroughly 'checked you out.' Therefore my behavior—body language, responses to the process, willingness to participate and be an active member (not quite peer but not distant professional either)—are critical to building an environment that will be conducive to sharing. Newly recovering alcoholics in a group are very nervous and fearful. I believe that they need to relax and feel 'welcomed' for trust to be established. If the 'professionals' who enter the room are as 'uptight' as they are, how can health happen? They 'feel' you right away. Therefore, how I feel about me sets the mood for the group and what will happen in the group.

"I believe, too, that what the best role model, the most 'comfortable-with-oneself' counselor, needs, especially with this population, is to be a rational, caring authoritarian. In many sessions I find myself setting limits. I do this always with open-ended groups where new members are constantly entering the group. In this kind of group, I quite often need to remind the members of the purpose, process, and rules of the group. I believe this offers them consistency and continuity. After the members reflect on that behavior of mine, I suspect that they view such discipline as empathic. They begin to view me as a role model, as somebody they want to be—strong yet caring, comfortable yet disciplined.

"I used the word 'rational' in the foregoing. I find that I often (but not too much) help patients to clarify what they are trying to say. In this context by 'rational' I mean that I help them to be concrete. I do not like to do this often, and when I help to clarify what they are saying, I try to clarify how I feel about what they are saying. Then I hope they can identify with how I could clarify what I felt. In a sense I try to identify with what they are trying to say and put that as succinctly as possible. I believe that everybody responds, in some way, to that which makes sense. This helps. It helps more if alcoholics can learn, and as succinctly as possible to put into words, how they feel about themselves for the purposes of growth and the more immediate purpose of stopping drinking. If alcoholics can do this themselves, their chances of gaining lasting insight are greatly enhanced. I believe that insight will last and have a more powerful effect if it is discovered through self-examination, and verbalized out loud within a group of peers attempting to do the same thing. What I am saying is that in a group, rational, concrete, make-sense insights discovered by the individual, stimulated by the group, are very potent. They provide the foundation for change that lasts.

"A group therapist being a role model, being rational and empathic and tempering this givingness with authority and discipline, needs more—to be 'right there,' not to wait to show feelings about a discovered insight by a group member or a certain behavior displayed by an individual. The therapist needs to intervene immediately in a crisis or discipline an unacceptable behavior. I believe the effect of modifying one's behavior will be lost if the intervener (in this case the group therapist) waits to interpret his approval or disapproval or insights in response to a behavior of a client or subgroup of clients. What could be worse than waiting is the group therapist not responding at all. It is difficult to describe when or how to do these kinds of things. They are not quantifiable. They are judgment calls. Surely it would be impossible to describe every instance that arises in a group. One must be spontaneous and respond in some noticeable way. Reacting emotionally is O.K. If it is honest, it can be beneficial. If you become angry, be angry. I seek to teach people how to cummunicate, how to react positively to their feelings, the rewards, benefits, and difficulties related to communication. If I become angry and do not express that emotion, how honestly human am I being? Am I being a good role model or a hypocrite?

"Despite all this, we *are* professionals. Therefore, we are to help our clients, not ourselves. So our opinions and our feelings are important if we are clear, if these 'displayed emotions' make sense and have a purpose. That purpose must be solely to help our clients. The only instance that I have ever seen to the contrary was when a colleague of mine 'mildly exploded' because his group for four weeks displayed no motivation for change (many of the members were coerced into treatment by the judicial system), were lethargic and waiting to be entertained. In this instance I feel that not to respond in any way to that kind of apathy would not be beneficial for the clients. They at least got the message that their group leader felt change for 'problem drinkers' is important and *their* responsibility. Again, such behavior is tricky, and requires skill, experience, and a good sense of judgment.

"For us to be clear, we must understand the feelings behind the faces. We must be able accurately to recognize symptoms, that is, fear, anxiety, panic, etc., and to make a scientifically based guess as to their etiology. A group therapist must be thinking constantly about the dynamics that are taking place, the energy that each group member is expelling (whether it be deep emotion or withdrawn lethargy). The therapist must be able to answer the questions: How is the energy that the client is releasing causing change? Is it a positive change or is it causing ego decompensation? A good therapist can precisely understand and make a logical, scientific (based on theory) guess at the best way to direct the group.

In the navigation of the group, a good therapist will not waste time—will not travel in waters that need not be traveled or enter ports the client might not want to leave. At the same time, for purposes of lasting insight some clients will probably be allowed to struggle with each other. When that happens I am clear and direct when I say anything. I find that if I am not, then I run the risk of losing credibility. I must always remember that I am a role model.

"In sum, then, to be an effective group therapist one must know oneself very well. It is only through knowing oneself that a person can really learn to listen to the 'energy' that is being released by individuals. Newly recovering alcoholics are individuals who are hypersensitive, whose ego controls are as fragile as the paper on which we write our progress notes.

"An effective group therapist needs to be as honest as possible and needs to be able to interpret personal feelings and know what the process feels like. The therapist must be able to express those feelings only when it will benefit the members of the group. Obviously this requires sound judgment. The process of self-examination will by itself create sound judgment.

"I believe the above because it is only through experiencing self-examination that one can best teach others the process. Self-examination will lead to emotional health, which in turn means to find alternatives that will enhance oneself and cause one to feel the courage to pursue that often frightening, newly discovered alternative. To share the experience of self-examination accurately, and almost to insist that people learn it, is a noble but often excruciating task. This is so because what we are really doing is teaching alcoholics to become comfortable with who they are and to do it without alcohol. The only means that I know to do this is to encourage them to talk about themselves.

"Honesty, patience, discipline, strength (being aware of one's own needs—countertransference issues), and good judgment are some of the fundamental qualities that make a good group therapist. Incorporating these qualities into one's personal life, living the messages that a therapist gives clients, are critical for them to observe. It is for this reason that I believe that being a 'role model' is a fundamental quality for an effective group therapist.

"Throughout my 'opinion' of what makes an effective group therapist, and in terms of group operations, I used words such as rational and concrete and such phrases as 'being able to deliver these messages to the group through precise language (body or verbal).' As was stated several times, these kinds of things will have to be genuine, and even then there will be resistance. One must live the life of constant self-examination if one is to teach it, and if one is to be effective with the alcoholic population as a group therapist."

2. *Female, 39 years old, 14 years' experience as a group counselor, Ph.D., recovering alcoholic.*

"This question of effective qualities deals with two counselors: the counselor as a person and the counselor as a professional. In alcoholism counseling person and professional blend. What I'm saying is that the qualities that make for a successful (I don't like 'effective' in this context; it's jargonistic) alcoholism counselor are the same ones that make for a successful human being. There are three: authenticity, approachability, and empathy.

"An authentic person battles against phoniness every moment of his or her waking life. An authentic person is ever alert not to *think* phoney. Our personal dishonesties are the source of all our problems, and they all really start there—in our thoughts. When we refuse or are unable to see ourselves as the really beautiful people we are, we are thinking phoney. When we envy someone else, we are thinking phoney. When we try to act like someone else, someone 'sophisticated,' it's because we are thinking phoney. When we put ourselves under useless anxiety, it's because we are thinking phoney. The road to alcoholism and addictions of all kinds is paved with phoney thinkers. The road to sobriety is paved with authentic thinkers.

"Authenticity makes for approachability. An alcoholism counselor must ever be approachable to be able to serve clients. The approachable counselor wears approachability all over the body. The way of walking, sitting, standing and talking tells clients that the counselor is there to help them back to health.

"A successful counselor must be empathic. I say 'must be' because I can't understand how any counselor can ever become emotionally close to a client without this quality. I'm convinced that it's the quality among alcoholics that helps us see and root out the phoniness in each other."

3. *Male, 42 years old, two years' experience as a group counselor, M.A., recovering alcoholic.*

"The group counselor in the alcoholic rehabilitation setting must have personal characteristics analogous to those of a playwright.

The playwright must be perceptive enough to discern hidden meanings in both the speech and manner of people and must have an ability to assess accurately the true meaning of speech and manner when distorted consciously or unconsciously by the persons being seen and listened to. This same quality is essential to the group counselor who must hear or see the false note, gauge the real meaning, and sense the truth.

"The playwright must observe each little nuance of nonverbal behavior so as not to sacrifice a full understanding of characters by limiting their ability to communicate to a vocabulary. The group counslor must possess the same keen eye for nuance and have the ability to know the message it conveys as clearly as the spoken word.

"The playwright must put characters together in such a way that they create conflict, confront conflict, and resolve conflict in a credible, deep, and enduring way. And so must the group counselor guide his or her characters together, unearthing conflict, confronting conflict, and resolving conflict in a productive and enduring way.

"The playwright has a message or messages to convey. But all is lost if the playwright simply walks on the stage and announces the message. The message only becomes real and clear and enduring as it unfolds through the actors in the play. And so must the group counselor let the story of the denial, rationalization, projection, avoidance, withdrawal, and regression tell itself through the actors in the group for the fullest impact. The play is indeed the thing.

"Shaw said, 'My fiction is the lie I tell you to explain the truth' The writer is redefining reality in personal terms and making it believable to an audience willing to suspend belief. The group counselor, employing the same qualities and skills, has the same goal—to explain the truth.

"But the method is exactly the opposite. The group counselor begins with an audience that has already redefined reality in a most distorted way. The goal is to get them to face reality and accept it as it is and to surrender the redefinition of their own that protects them from truth. The group counselor must work not with people who have agreed temporarily to suspend disbelief, but with people who are rooted in disbelief and mistrust—people who must be willing instead to believe.

"To accomplish all this, the group counselor needs to pay heed to—no, to live—the ancient dictum, 'Know thyself.' "

Integration of the Responses

If there is a common message in the three counselors' views, it is this: An effective group counselor is a person vitally concerned with the welfare of his or her clients. The counselor's basic function is to be "right there," to "be approachable," to explain the truth to people rooted in disbelief and mistrust.

The first two counselors believe that the fastest, surest road to authenticity lies in self-examination, in getting to know oneself. The third counselor stresses a keen perception and an exquisite sensitivity as the qualities necessary to be an effective group counselor. In his "a keen eye for nuance" and the ability to "discern hidden meanings" are competencies that can only enhance the group.

Finally and most important, the quality that comes forth brilliantly in all three presentations is thoughtfulness. Apparently these counselors have a strong bent for introspection. If nothing else, their responses tell us that before we can competently understand and interpret the dynamics of our clients, we must first have a full appreciation of what our own are. Thus the first counselor tells us "How I feel about me sets the mood for the group and what will happen in the group." The second writes, "When we refuse or are unable to see ourselves as the really beautiful people we are, we are thinking phoney." The third puts it nicely indeed: "The group counselor needs to pay heed to—no, to live—the ancient dictim, 'Know thyself.'"

COUNSELOR FUNCTIONS

COUNSELORS HAVE two functions. One is administrative, the other is therapeutic. How much importance, time, and attention counselors wish to attach to the first will be determined by their disposition and preference. Some counselors are careful to keep the two functions separate; others ignore or blend the administrative with the therapeutic.

Administrative Functions

The first administrative function has to do with the *collection of information*. Counselors' opinions vary as to how well a counselor should know the group members. Stoller (1968) believes that prior information on clients might "dilute the impact that the individual makes within the situation" (p. 62). Hansen and colleagues (1976) believe just the opposite. Thus they wrote that prospective participants of a group "should be thoroughly screened so that the counselor will understand as much as possible about them" (p. 363). Trotzer (1977) believes that members should be interviewed on an individual basis. The focus of the interview "should be (1) client expectations, (2) counselor assessment, and (3) client commitment" (p. 180). This author, like Trotzer and Hansen et al., believes that the counselor should have as much information as possible about each prospective group member. The author's experience has been that progress and success with a group are in direct proportion to how well he knows them. Prior information about group members only facilitated getting to know them.

Knowledge about a member's current status in each of the following areas has proved particularly valuable: health, law, intragroup relationships, and prior and current counseling contacts.

It is important to know the history and have information about the current health (both medical and psychological) of any prospective group members. The counselor should know whether any of the clients were ever hospitalized for alcoholism and if any are on medication.

Counselors should inquire into the legal history and status of their group members. A disproportionate number of alcoholic group members have been law offenders. Many of this counselor's clients have been arrested for such offenses as driving under the influence, disturbing the peace, and assault and battery. Usually these occurred because and while they were drunk. Not uncommonly, their entry into the group is on the recommendation or order of the court.

Sometimes group members are involved in drug trafficking. It is best not to admit such members into group because if they should reveal such information in a group session, peer members, who are bound to the rule of confidentiality, will be put under an onus that they should not have to carry.

The counselor should know whether two members of a given group are or have been involved in an intimate relationship. Not long ago this counselor had two members in an alcoholic group who had had a brief homosexual affair prior to the formation of the group. One of them was still embittered about its outcome. He recognized that the group was not the setting in which to come to a resolution of his feelings, and dropped out at the second meeting. What this counselor learned from this experience was that although there is actually little one can do about it, counselors should discourage the after-hours cultivation of close relationships between group members. More often than not, such relationships militate against group cohesion and progress.

Counselors should always know if participants are in counseling (individual, couple, or group) elsewhere. They should know how long such counseling has been going on and, with the client, assess whether or not it can complement or work against the group.

The second administrative function has to do with *launching and hosting the group.* Group leaders are, by definition, in charge. They "cannot shirk the assigned task of organizing and launching the group" (Dinkmeyer & Muro, 1979, p. 63). Among the necessary tasks involved in launching and then hosting the group are:

1. Coordinating a meeting time and place.
2. Explaining group rules.
3. Explaining basic roles.

The task that most counselors find frustrating and exasperating is that of arranging a meeting time for group members. Everybody wants the most convenient time. Indeed compromise on time coordination for a group is as likely to bring about hostility as to abate it.

At the first session, the leader ordinarily points out some of the basic rules of the group. Members are told that they are not to talk *about* each other to the leader or another member but are to talk *to* each other. It is also pointed out that interrupting the leader or another member is not appropriate. Smoking, coffee drinking, and eating are usually permitted, as is walking around. If this is a group's first session, the leader introduces each member. If it is a new member's first session, the leader introduces him or her. New members are acclimated quickly to the group. At the first session of a totally new group, members are asked to tell what they expect to derive from the group. They are asked to establish a goal for each subsequent session, which they learn to state routinely. These specifics for hosting and launching the group are ones that the author uses. They may not suit the reader. This is understandable as leaders should launch and host a group in terms of what fits their own personality and rationale.

The task of explaining roles and their consequent obligation is important, even critical, especially for those who have never previously been members of an alcoholic group. This should be done at the first meeting. Clients must know that their responsibilities as members of the group are to listen, share, respond, and self-disclose. Confrontations and interpretations are better left to the leader. Unfortunately, most new members believe that confrontations liberally spiced with interpretations are the prime, if not the exclusive, concern in group counseling. Despite such explanations members continue to interpret for each other. Ironically, what counselors learn is that the interpretations, especially in the latter stages of the group, are excellent.

Therapeutic Functions

Many of the techniques and skills described in Chapter VI are incorporated in the four major therapeutic functions: defending, supporting, observing, and intervening.

Alcoholism groups invariably have one or more members who fluctuate widely in mood and disposition regarding others. These moods range from quiet inhibition to vitriolic hostility. When in the latter mood, they could, if left alone, brutalize other members. This is when the leader becomes involved in *defending* the other members. This can be done with an ironic comment, "Jack, I think you already asked Mike if he was drinking." Or much better, with an invitation to another member to participate and thereby insulate Mike from Jack's foul mood. The invitation can be framed as a simple question, "What do you think about all this, Martin?" The trick is to be sure that Martin is the type who likes to explain what he thinks.

Another major counselor function is *supporting*. It is through this function particularly that the counselor rewards and encourages the shy, inhibited, sometimes scared individual, who finds it so difficult to participate and self-disclose. Facial expressions communicating acceptance and receptivity, a smile and nod, speak support as well as do words of encouragement. Again, the most important aspect of this function for the counselor is to know when to use it and who among the members needs it.

That group counselor who functions best is constantly *observing* all that is going on. Observing is not just a visual function; it is an emotional one as well. Observing has to do as much with being emotionally attuned to the tone nuances of a particular member as noticing that Ellen has a new hair style. The observing counselor is the one who has emotional antennae out and receiving throughout the session. Observing, then, is both a conscious and unconscious process—and it is constant. Alcoholics in group invariably react negatively to the counselor who is not observing or who lapses. Why? The answer is that alcoholics generally interpret the nonobserving counselor as lacking in interest and concern. Observing is an integral function and if it is not done and well, the function of intervening cannot proceed.

Intervening is at the heart of the group process. When counselors intervene, they share their skills with the group. These skills involve such techniques as listening, questioning, clarifying client feeling, reflecting feeling (they mirror the client's feelings), recapitulating, and confronting. (See Chapter VI.)

What invariably happens in the group that attains cohesion and progresses is that the members themselves begin to use these newly learned techniques on each other and on the leader. And this is as it should be. There is no better compliment to a leader than to see a member mirror feelings to a peer. What such behavior shows is that members are learning from the leader to give and share with other members.

COUNSELOR TRAINING

Research Findings

Research findings support the idea that the time and money spent on training programs are worthwhile. In a study with 16 female alcoholics who became counselors, Hoffmann and Bonyge (1977) found that the training had beneficial effects. Over the course of nine months, in a curriculum that focused on personal confrontation and self-awareness, the women became more task-oriented and generally more accepting of others. Skuja and colleagues (1975) evaluated the effects of a shorter but more intense program upon 41 alcoholism trainees. These researchers found that after seven weeks, and again after 14 weeks, the general level of trainee competency increased. These increases were especially marked in personal involvement, responsibility, alcoholism utilization, and overall job performance. Wehler and Hoffman (1978) did a pretest and posttest study with 14 female alcoholism counselors who underwent a nine-month training program. These researchers found that when they had completed the program, the women showed increased general spontaneity, the ability to get closer to people, stronger and more positive feelings about themselves, and easier and more feeling reactions to others. Most important of all, the subjects in the study had developed a stronger penchant for self-actualization.

A Survey and Discussion

The author conducted a mail survey of 23 alcoholism treatment centers located in five New England states and New York. His findings were that:

1. Counseling in-service training is an integral part of total activity.
2. Training in group counseling is an aspect of all training programs.
3. Group training for novice counselors varies considerably in both depth and time.
4. Group training focuses on practical in-contact experience, *not* didactic instruction.
5. Attendance of academic workshops, credit courses, and degree programs is encouraged, sometimes even supported by allowing counselors time off from work or by full or partial tuition reimbursement.

The training of alcoholism counselors for group work is regarded as a desirable and important activity. At the same time, there are few, if any, standards with respect to the scope and depth of that training. Alcoholism counselors, for whatever reasons, seem to shy away from development of solid theoretical foundations for their work with groups. Paradoxically virtually every institution sampled supported participation in college work.

These findings were not surprising. They are perfectly consistent with the history and development of alcoholism counseling. Alcoholism counselors traditionally have been, and continue to be, recovering alcoholics. Only a minority have any formal education in counseling theory. The education in most cases has little to do theoretically, or even practically, with the helping professions.

The author is neither alarmed nor discouraged by any of this. He learned long ago that academic credentials do not a counselor make. He agrees heartily with Werry's (1968) view that "the most important determinant of the therapist's effectiveness lies in his personality, his capacity to empathize with the patient" (p. 7). The issue, in short and finally, has to do not with credentials, but with effectiveness. Haley (1971) put it succinctly when he wrote, "A therapist is now often judged on his merit—the success of his therapy—not upon his professional background'' (p. 284). Haley was discussing family therapists, but such a view finds favor with the counselors of alcoholic groups. By and large this is all alcoholism counselors want—success in their therapy. It is the only way that they can help their clients achieve and maintain sobriety.

It is obvious that alcoholism counselors are not motivated by the financial rewards. The salaries of group counselors of alcoholics are pitifully low. In some cases there is no salary at all (church groups and local AA organizations). The motive for the vast majority of alcoholism counselors, is the success of their therapy.

This motive explains why counselors are attracted to and focus upon the practical rather than the theoretical aspects of training—on interactive experience with their clients. Such experience is more readily understood and seems to yield fruits more quickly not only for their clients, but for themselves as well. Counselors themselves feel as though they grow personally through the group experience.

This interest in personal growth helps to explain why counselors pursue learning their skills by interpersonal activities rather than formal degree programs. For alcoholism counselors the value and status of learning lie not in transcripts or diplomas, but in knowing and being skillful with their groups. Such a view is healthy because it directly benefits the client. And it is healthy for another reason. It provides the common ground for communication among counselors whose education ranges from grade to graduate school and who come from the broadest spectrum of vocations.

A counseling staff is usually made up of nurses, psychologists, social workers, and physicians. Typically these professionals form only the inner core of an institutional staff. There are, in addition, those people called ''counselors''—the ones who, by and large, have the most contact hours with the alcoholic, in both group and individual counseling. Although some of them have impeccable counseling credentials, most have none at all, yet they function at least satisfactorily with their clients, and some function very well. There are two reasons for this, and both lie in Werry's observation that a counselor's competence is a function of personality and the ability to empathize. People without a counseling background who apply for positions as alcoholism counselors are themselves alcoholics who are recovering. They are people who have learned from their alcoholism. They derived profound personal meanings from the pain of their experiences. The meanings usually center on an understanding of the whys of their lives and their relationships with others. Recovering alcoholics who counsel do so because they derive rich personal dividends from their investment in others. There is little doubt that such a motive effected the findings of two alcoholism researchers (Argeriou & Manohar, 1978). Their work uncovered the fact that alcoholics who were in the recovery process were far more effective with youthful drinkers than were better trained but nonalcoholic counselors. These findings were corroborated in a subsequent study by Lawson (1982), who found that the counselor who has experienced a period of alcoholism will be better equipped to develop a therapeutic relationship with alcoholic clients.

One is not to conclude from these studies that nonalcoholics cannot be effective alcoholism counselors. Just as one does not have to experience a terminal disease to have an emotional appreciation of its destructiveness, one does not have to experience alcoholism to empathize with the alcoholic.

At the same time, to the nonalcoholic counselor there often seems to be a club among the recovering alcoholics. They seem to have an uncanny bond of understanding. Although unspoken, it seems to be instant. In group it is real.

This bond stems from the need to escape from the constant, latent sense of aloneness with which alcoholics live, wet or sober. With the emotional commitment to stop drinking, the aloneness becomes even more acute. Entry into the group provides them with a real opportunity to mitigate the aloneness and to feed the strong need for perceptual camaraderie, to share with one "who has been there." It is for these reasons that the alcoholic will more readily accept empathy from the counselor who is recovering.

Functional Programs

In one of the earliest descriptions of an alcoholism training program, Wilson (1968) recommended that counselors be trained not only in the traditional individual counseling, but also in group counseling. Use of the videotape, he felt, could help facilitate such training.

Learning to lead a group is a skill that can be acquired by both new incoming staff and volunteers. Manohar (1973) describes a program for training volunteers to work as alcoholism treatment counselors. Following ten weeks of academic work, the volunteers spend 40 hours per week for 50 weeks in an alcoholism treatment center under professional supervision. During the 40 hours per week, volunteers also attend staff meetings and professional seminars.

For the past decade, the trend has been toward developing competency-oriented programs. This trend is in response to the acute need for counselors generally. The state of Washington was the first to implement this kind of a program. Performance objectives are established and defined. Prospective counselors apply and are assessed. The decision is then made whether to recommend or deny certification. Counselors who are recommended enter into a lifelong professional development work situation. Those who are denied can choose to enter a skill training program. At its completion they are reassessed, and if recommended, become state certified (Brammer & Springer, 1971).

Another impressive program is the one described by Constantine (1976), which was implemented at Boston State Hospital. It is a program that was designed for family therapists but can easily be adapted for group alcoholism counselors. Prospective counselors are drawn from different professions and levels of skill. They include both psychiatrists and mental health aides. The program lasts two years. The first year is divided into four sequential units. The curriculum is designed to prepare the prospective counselors for their first group experience, which occurs near the end of the first year. The administrators of this program do not believe in the "sink or swim approach" found in some alcoholism centers. During the second year, the trainee counselors are given more and more responsibility and groups until they are treating a minimum of three groups.

Training Recommendations

A three-day workshop is suggested, as outlined in the following.

Time 9 A.M. to 4 P.M.

Number of participants Minimum, 7; maximum, 12.

Criteria for admission Experience as an alcoholism counselor.

Objective To help participants sharpen group counseling skills.

Procedural activities

Days 1 and 2—Morning and afternoon

Participants are divided into two or more groups so that each member can be videotaped leading a group for approximately 50 minutes. Members are then critiqued by the group on their skill in utilizing each of the following techniques.

1. Confronting.
2. Questioning.
3. Probing.
4. Self-disclosing.
5. Reiterating.
6. Clarifying.
7. Reflecting.
8. Recapitulating.
9. Listening.

Day 3: Morning and afternoon

Reactions to preceding day's agenda explored. If group chooses, the balance of the morning is spent in completion of that agenda. Otherwise the leader introduces for discussion, and where appropriate demonstrates by role playing with selected members, behaviors commonly encountered. These include:

1. Absence.
2. Withdrawal.
3. Silence.
4. Intellectualization.
5. Hostility.
6. Professionalizing.
7. Manipulation.
8. Housekeeping.
9. Clowning

During the last hour, members are asked to write evaluations of the leader of the workshop. Specifically they are asked to consider the following questions.

1. How was the leader an effective facilitator for cohesion? How not?
2. Was the choice of curriculum valuable for you? If so, why? If not, why not?
3. Was the leader approachable? What interpersonal qualities made the leader so? What made the leader unapproachable?

The following synopsis was prepared for a course in a sequence of offerings as part of a program leading to a certificate in alcoholism counseling. The maximum number permitted to enroll was 12.

Counseling the Alcoholic Group—A Synopsis

Objective To be able to counsel an alcoholic group.

Prerequisites Theories of group counseling or experience in alcoholism counseling.

Methodolgy Lecture, discussion, and practica.

Curriculum During first four weeks, instructor will lecture on:

1. Dynamics of the alcoholic group.
2. Qualities that make for an effective alcoholism counselor.
3. Group member behaviors.
4. Stages of group process.
5. Counselor techniques of action and reaction.
6. Activities in an alcoholic group.

Concurently with lectures (four weeks), students will spend two hours per week observing a counselor leading an alcoholic group.

During the balance of the course (ten weeks), students will cofacilitate an alcoholic group with a mentor–counselor and will have prepared three videotapes of them leading an alcoholic group with their mentor present. One tape will be critiqued in class, the others by the instructor alone.

Texts *Counseling the Alcoholic,* by J. F. Perez *Counseling the Alcoholic Group* by J. F. Perez

Criteria for grade:

Performance on written exam.

Performance on tapes.

Mentor–counselor evaluation.

YOU, THE NEW GROUP COUNSELOR

Some Personal Thoughts

How you lead your group finally is a function of you. Counseling is a very personal experience and the meanings that you derive from each experience are yours and yours alone. Those meanings are critical as they will determine how optimistically or pessimistically you will perceive the next session. Be aware! How you perceive the group will determine how it will go—toward health or toward dissolution.

Trust the feelings you have at the end of a session. They are the best criteria for trying to determine how good or bad a session was. They are almost always right. Welcome those feelings of contentment and exhilaration. You did well! And do not discount or ignore those queasy feelings of dissatisfaction or that constant nagging feeling that you missed something important. Bank on it. You did.

If those last kinds of feelings bother you, take heart. It means you have a conscience, that you are dedicated, that you want to be good, you want to do well. Remember, only this kind of person can succeed as a group counselor.

All of the research material and explanations presented here are presented for your examination. What you accept and what you reject are a function of what fits and works into your developing rationale for counseling, and this you must have so that you can articulate why you do what you do in group. Far more important, you must have a rationale to satisfy your personal sense of authenticity. In short, you have to have a clear intellectual understanding and emotional appreciation of *why* you do what you do. If you do not, you are a fool, or worse, a charlatan. Since you are neither, consider the following list of questions. They are designed to help you develop your rationale.

Guidelines of Rationale

Professional Criteria

1. What is your definition of counseling the alcoholic group?
2. How would you define your role as group counselor?

3. What are your most important functions as a group counselor?

4. What are the personal and professional qualities that make for a competent group counselor?

5. What distinguishes a mediocre from an outstanding group therapist?

Personal Criteria

1. What are the main values you live by? How do these values help/hurt your work in the group?

2. What are your values concerning the following?

   a. Religion, politics, the opposite sex.

   b. Sex outside of marriage, abortion, marriage, homosexuality.

   c. Drugs.

3. Can any of these hinder you in your work as a group counselor?

4. How would you define or describe "the good life?"

5. Why do you choose to be a group counselor of alcoholics? What is in it for you personally?

5. What needs of yours are being met by being a group alcoholism counselor?

6. How do you view your level of functioning?

7. What makes you think you can be of value in helping alcoholics achieve and maintain sobriety?

SUMMARY

THE RESEARCH shows that counselors who perceive their clients optimistically will be more successful with them. Such success is also affected by counselors' values and ethics. Important among these appear to be a need to help others, a willingness to take risks in the counseling process, and flexibility.

Three experienced counselors presented the view that an effective group counselor is a person vitally concerned with the welfare of his or her clients. These counselors showed themselves to be thoughtful and with a strong bent for introspection. One of their messages was; Before we can understand and competently interpret the dynamics of our clients, we must first have a full appreciation of what our own are.

The counselor's functions are twofold. The administrative function includes collecting information and launching and hosting the group. The therapeutic function includes defending, supporting, observing, and intervening.

The time and money spent on training are worthwhile. In-service training is an integral part of total activity. Group training is an aspect of all training programs and varies in both depth and time for novice counselors. It focuses on practical in-contact experience, which alcoholism counselors seem to prefer. Competency-based programs seem to be a developing trend and the one implemented at Boston State Hospital is adaptable for group work with alcoholics.

New counselors will need to develop a clear rationale for their counseling if they are to function successfully with their group. The criteria for such a rationale are both professional and personal.

REFERENCES

Argeriou, M., and Manohar, V. Relative effectiveness of non-alcoholics and recovered alcoholics as counselors *J Stud Alc.* 39(5): 793–799, 1978.

Brammer, L. M. and Springer, H. C. A radical change in counselor education and certification *Personnel Guide Jo*49: 806, June 1971.

Constantine, L. L. Designed experience: A multiple, goal directed training program in family therapy. *Fam Proc,* 15:373–387, 1976.

Dinkmeyer, D. C., and Muro, J. J. *Group Counseling,* 2nd ed. Itasca, Ill.: Peacock, 1979, p. 63.

Haley, J. Family Therapy: A radical change. In Changing Families: A Family Therapy Reader. New York: Grune & Stratton, 1971, p. 284.

Hansen, J. C., Warner, R. W., and Smith, E. M. *Group Counseling: Theory and Process.* Chicago: Rand-McNally, 1976, p. 363.

Hart, L. Attitudes toward Alcoholism Among a group of rehabilitation counselors: An exploratory study. *Drug Forum* 5(2):139–142, 1975–76.

Hertzman, M., and Mitnick, L. Ethics, evaluation and training in alcoholism. *Drug Forum* 7(2):145–154, 1978–79.

Hoffmann, H., and Bonyge, E. R. Personalities of female alcoholics who became counselors. *Psychol Rep* 41(1): 37–38, 1977.

Lawson, G. Relation of counselor traits to evaluation of the counseling relationship by alcoholics. *J Stud Alc* 43:834–839, 1982.

Leake, G., and King, A. Effect of counselor expectations on alcoholic recovery, *Alc Health Res World* 1(3):16–22, 1977.

Manohar, V. Training volunteers as alcoholism treatment counselors. *J Stud Alc* 34(3):869–877, 1973.

Menne, J. M. A comprehensive set of counselor competencies. *J Couns Psychol* 22:547–553, 1975.

Perez, J. F. *Family Counseling: Theory and Practice.* New York: Van Nostrand, 1979, pp 87–88.

Perez, J. F. *Counseling the Alcoholic.* Muncie, Ind.: Accelerated Development, 1985, pp. 65–77

Rutan, J. S., and Rice, C. A. The charismatic leader: Asset or liability? *Psychother: Theory Res Prac* 18(14):487–492, 1981.

Scheid, A. B. Client's perception of the counselor. The influence of counselor introduction and behavior. *J Couns Psychol* 23:505–508, 1976.

Skuja, A. T., Schneidmuhl, A. M., and Mandell, W. Alcoholism counselor trainees: Some changes in job related functioning following training. *J. Drug Ed* 5(2):151–157, 1975.

Stoller, F. Marathon group therapy. In G. Gazda (ed.), *Innovations to Group Psychotherapy.* Springfield, Ill.: Charles C. Thomas, 1968, p. 62.

Talbot, J., and Gillen, C. Differences between nonprofessional recovering alcoholic counselors treating bowery alcoholics: A study of therapist variables. *Psychiat Q* 50(4):333–342, 1978.

Trotzer, J. P. *The Counselor and the Group: Integrating Theory, Training and Practice.* Monterey, Calif.: Brooks/Cole, 1977, p. 180.

Valle, S. K. Interpersonal functioning of alcoholism counselors and treatment outcome. *J Stud Alc* 42:783–790, 1981.

Wehler, R., and Hoffmann, J. Personal orientation inventory scores of female alcoholism counselors before and after training. *Psychol Rep* 43(2):500–502, 1978.

Werry, J. S. The psychiatrist and society. *Dis-Coverer,* 5(3):1–12, 1968. (The 1967 Velde Lecture, Bradley University, Peoria, Ill., Apr. 26–27.)

Wile, D. B. Personality styles and therapy styles. *Psychother: Theory Res Prac* 13:303–307, 1976.

Wilson, W. M. Hospitalized alcoholic patients: Training personnel to work with alcoholic patients. *Hosp Commun Psychiat* 19(7):211–215, 1968.

Chapter V

The Group: Theoretical Considerations

SELECTION AND COMPOSITION

A CRITICAL FACTOR in how successful a group will be is its composition. Ideally counselors should be able to establish criteria for the selection of a group's members. By doing so they not only will be structuring for group success but they will also increase the probability that members will profit. The author is very much aware that alcoholism counselors sometimes are not afforded the luxury of selecting their members because of the pressure of administrative obligations and numbers to be treated. Nonetheless it is sometimes possible to do so. When this is the case, the following criteria should be employed.

1. Readiness for the group.
2. Level of articulation.
3. Client expectations about success.
4. Disposition to help others.
5. Sexual heterogeneity.

Each alcoholic admitted to the group should be motivated to be a member. Self-referred individuals are to be preferred (Rickard, 1965); court-mandated referrals are not. When alcoholics seek counseling because of externally applied pressure rather than an internally felt desire, the prospects for significant benefits are at best minimal.

Group counseling is fundamentally a verbal process. Individuals who have difficulty articulating are not as likely to profit from the group as are those who do not. If a person is not verbally oriented or inclined, group interaction will be painful and embarrassing even before exploration of personal problems begins. Bach (1954) feels such people will be made to feel frustrated and uncomfortable, especially if some in the group are unusually articulate. In such a situation, feelings of inadequacy (rampant among alcoholics) can only be fueled. Individual counseling might be a better alternative for these alcoholics.

At the very least, alcoholics should be open minded about the benefits they expect to derive from the group. If their expectations are low, the possibility of benefits derived will be minimal. This concept is supported in the research of Truax and Carkhuff (1967, Chap. 5), who found that when client expectations are that there will be help in group counseling this is a critical factor in whether or not it will be obtained.

Potential members whose talk or past behavior reflects an interest in helping others are excellent candidates for group. As was noted in both Chapter II and Chapter III, the member who is inclined toward the sublimation defense is one who will enhance the group.

Sadock and Kaplan (1972) believe that whenever possible a group should contain both men and women. Their view is that such a group provides a more normal climate than with members of only one sex. This author concurs. Sexual heterogeneity in the alcoholic group is highly desirable. The interaction afforded by the group should prove beneficial as a common deficiency found among both male and female alcoholics is their lack of self-esteem in dealing with the other sex.

RAPPORT

Rapport in group may be defined as a *working relationship* between leader and members and among the members. While the presence of warmth and affinity can and does facilitate rapport, it is not an indispensable prerequisite. Rapport in the alcoholic group is founded not upon the personal warmth and affinity of counselor and members as in individual counseling, but upon predictability and security of mutual help. Many alcoholics come to group to help, and are themselves helped, but still maintain a facade of coolness and distance throughout their tenure in group. The reason is that alcoholics know that the final responsibility to achieve and maintain their sobriety lies within themselves exclusively—not in a relationship. Group relationships are usually fleeting. The self-knowledge that each member seeks to achieve and maintain as the goal of sobriety must be the prime concern. Members are important to each other only to learn about themselves. The members' need of each other and of the counselor is founded on attaining the emotional and mental impetus to stay sober. Rapport in the alcoholic group need only be practical and utilitarian; it does not have to be warmly interpersonal to be effective.

This is not to say that the counselor cannot establish rapport of the quality found in individual counseling with many members. Nor does it mean that many members cannot do the same among themselves—and many do. However, many do not and still derive a great deal of benefit from the group.

Establishment

This working relationship can be established at the initial contact once these requirements are met.

1. Counselor competence.
2. An explanation of roles and responsibilities.

Counselors who are competent show it because they feel they are. Such feelings are usually a function of both personality and training. Feelings of confidence are important because they are inevitably transmitted to the group. At first meetings alcoholics search long and hard to assess how confident a counselor is. Why? They are coming for help. They are skeptical and they are scared. Personal confidence is a sought-after commodity. They desperately want to identify with it. In short, the counselor who communicates confidence facilitates rapport within the group.

At the initial contact, counselors should explain their roles and responsibilities and those of the members' (see "Administrative Functions", Chapter IV). It is precisely here that counselors are able to communicate confidence. Their words, affect, and body language are all key elements in delivery. How effectively they communicate confidence sets the stage for the quality of rapport in group and thereby the degree of therapeutic progress.

A short time ago, and because he knew he would be writing this section on rapport, the author taped himself with a newly formed group of college-aged children of alcoholics (some of whom were alcoholics themselves). Each of the ten members had volunteered and had been interviewed briefly.

"What do we do here? Not hard for some. Very hard for others. You talk. When one of you is talking, we all listen. What do you talk about? You talk about your fear of alcohol and how it's screwed up your lives, and how you don't want it to in the future. You talk about what you have to do to control your own lives. That's what you do. In the process of doing all that you'll find yourselves telling, sharing a lot of stuff that you never did. Embarrassing stuff. That process usually makes you feel better afterward.

"Now if you cooperate and talk and share, you'll be helping me to help you."

(Question was asked) "How?"

"By listening. My job here is to listen and respond to what you say. In fact, each of you can do that, help by listening and responding if you think it's appropriate. If you do that, you're going to find something interesting happening. You're going to help yourselves as much as you think you're helping the other person. My recommendation, and I honestly believe your obligation in being here, is to try it. . . ."

Obstacles to Its Establishment

There are obstacles that can block establishment of rapport.

1. Counselor ego.
2. Unmotivated member.

3. Member's negative perception of the counselor.

Counselor Ego

Counselors who are unable to focus their complete attention on the group members will communicate that fact. Alcoholics will tend to read such behavior not only as a lack of interest but as a rejection of the group, and even of themselves particularly. The reality is, of course, that even a dedicated counselor's mind can wander. When it happens, as it might, the counselor should admit it, if asked, and even volunteer the fact if it seems appropriate. Under no circumstances should the counselor try to fudge the fact that he or she missed a point or simply was not attending. There is no surer way to block rapport establishment or maintenance, no surer way to fuel alcoholic paranoia.

The focusing of one's attention (essentially an aspect, but only one, of listening) is a skill. Some counselors find it inordinately difficult to learn it; others seem to have acquired it congenitally. In any case the effective counselors are those who have disciplined themselves to prevent and block irrelevant and distracting thoughts from interfering with counselor functions.

Counselors who harbor personal biases and are not able to comparmentalize them in group will not be able to establish rapport. Most notable among these would be intolerances of any kind—social, class, religious, ethnic, or nationality.

Counselors who are motivated to work with groups not so much to enhance and help but because they are on an ego trip will have a lot of difficulty relating to the group, let alone establishing rapport. Such counselors will be guilty of the cardinal sin of the group counselor—phoniness.

Unmotivated Member

Rapport is always difficult, and sometimes impossible, to establish when members (even one) are not motivated to participate. Unmotivated alcoholics are alcoholics who do not want to assume the responsibility to change, who basically want to hold on to their perception of themselves and of the world. Group counseling with such alcoholics is a waste of time. Indeed attempts at counseling only feed the alcoholics' dependency needs.

Negativism Toward Counselor

Sometimes the alcoholics' negative perception is limited to the group leader. Their problem is one of dealing with people whom *they* perceive to be in charge, in authority. The problem is not with the actual person who is the leader, but with the position. Alcoholics who perceive in this way do so usually because they themselves are authoritarian, perceiving a hostile, threatening world in which people want to control them. Such a perception by alcoholics can be ameliorated if the leader who is a recovering alcoholic lets that be known. Then the focus shifts from the leadership position to the person in that role. The leader is "one of their own." When the leader is not an alcoholic and the perception by one or more group members is negative, the leader should point out again that half of the responsibility to establish a working relationship belongs to the members; that members who cannot or who do not want to share responsibility are wasting their time.

What this author has found is that such confrontation generally has a positive impact. When it does not, it is usually because the member or members were not ready for the group.

SETTING

HOW PEOPLE PERCEIVE is affected by their physical environment. The classic study that demonstrates this was done by Maslow and Mintz in 1956. A follow-up was then carried out by Mintz (1956). These researchers discovered that perceptions are affected by the environment. They were found to be far more optimistic when the subjects were in attractive, newly decorated rooms than when they were in shabby rooms.

What this finding means for group counseling is that the money, time, and energy spent in making the meeting place attractive can only enhance the counseling process. Floors should be carpeted, and curtains and pictures hung. Colors should be muted rather than bombastic. Chaikin et al. (1976) found that how clients perceive a setting will influence how they perceive and thereby interact in counseling.

Research also shows that the amount of space that people are allowed affects how much they will self-disclose and for how long they will do so. Generally speaking, the larger the room, the more complete and the longer the duration of the self-disclosures (Haase & DiMattia, 1976). Another study, by Haase alone (1970), provides information as to how chairs should be spaced for a group. This researcher found that counseling participants, male and female, felt that a distance of 30–39 inches was about right. What makes this finding so interesting is that research by social psychologists has uncovered that this is the distance also preferred by intimate friends.

COMMUNICATION

Congruent Communication

Communication can take place at different levels: verbal, emotional, behavioral. Communication can be defined as congruent when all three levels come together. The affect expressed complements the words spoken and the language of the body. Drinking alcoholics do not communicate congruently. They cannot. Their emotional life is in disrepair. In group alcoholics who are in the BUD process also do not communicate congruently.

Alcoholics who communicate congruently are in a solid state of recovery. They do not speak idly. They look and apparently feel what they say. They volunteer and respond sensitively. They can say what is on their minds without offending.

Congruent communication enhances the person who speaks, the one spoken to, and the group in general. It is its own reward.

Body and Emotions

DeRivera's research has led him to believe that emotions and body are interwoven. Thus he wrote (DeRivera, 1977) that emotions "both influence the body and reflect the condition of the body" (p. 34). This conclusion supports the Szasz observations of a generation earlier that bodily symptoms are just another way in which the individual chooses to communicate. Symptoms, this psychiatrist wrote (Szasz, 1961, p. 302), are usually "cries for help." The alcoholic who continually reports new ailments at each session can be understood to be saying, "I'm confused. I'm in trouble. Help me!" Alcoholics who have been silent and finally begin to talk by discussing their physical ailments can be understood as testing the leader and the group for acceptance. If the leader and group are perceptive, they will respond positively and with sympathy. Such a response will inevitably move the physically ailing alcoholic to do what he or she wanted to do in the first place but was afraid to—discuss the real symptom, addiction to alcohol.

Unconscious Messages

Communication can occur on both the unconscious and the conscious level. Freud discovered this fact. The ego, he explained, wants to communicate a thought or feeling, but because of fear of possible reprisal from the superego or external reality, feels it cannot do so consciously. Thus to maintain its own integrity and still give the message, the ego relaxes its defenses, and with common forgetfulness behavior or the "verbal slip," the true feelings are released from the unconscious. Freud's admonition was that such messages had the greatest meaning and should be viewed as revealing the individual's true feelings. For example, he wrote that "the slip itself makes sense." Although the slip is unconscious, he regarded it "as a valid mental process following out its own purpose" (Freud, 1949, p. 33).

The existence of the slip is in itself a message, albeit a sad one. People have learned that they cannot always be open and honest, that expression of basic feelings sometimes has to be veiled by memory loss, an "unconscious" act or word. In short, people have learned to feel that sometimes it is more prudent *not* to be consciously direct and interpersonally honest. As children, many learn that expression of talk and feeling is inappropriate, irrelevant even, because others just do not listen—no one cares enough to listen. Later, for many of these people, a manifest symptom of this untalked-about early learning is alcoholism.

Group members who are constantly "slipping," who seldom talk "straight" or with candor, are usually those who underwent just such learning. These same people can make a dramatic improvement in their quality of talk and interaction once exposed to a caring leader and group members who do indeed listen.

Double Messages

As noted in Chapter II, alcoholics often take a suspicious view of the world. Such a perception can lead to a garbled system of communication usually characterized by double messages.

Double messages are messages in which words, affect, and behavior do not mesh. Examples of this in group might be the member who apologizes profusely for tardiness but continues to be tardy. Another might be the nonlistening member who promises to reform but continues to interrupt, yawn, or gaze out the window. Still another might be someone who disavows being hurt upon being chastised by the group, but then withdraws into silence.

Double messages militate against member and group health because they are dishonest. When the words spoken have one meaning and the behavior effected another, people can only become confused and anxious. The trust and openness so necessary in the counseling group are virtually impossible to promote in such a climate.

The best way to deal with double messages is to confront them. Leaders should never let them pass. Their inconsistencies should always be pointed out, examined, and the person responsible asked why. That person should be made to realize that double messages can only debilitate intragroup relationships.

Body Language

The body is a prime instrument for communication. How one *cares* for it and *uses* it communicate much about the person.

Alcoholics who attend a session ungroomed and looking or smelling as though they need a bath may be telling the group that they are on the skids, or at least that concern with self is not important. When self-concern is not prime, motivation for counseling is not usually prime either. Attendance at the sessions, however, can be viewed as a sign that some motivation still exists.

The irony about body care is that the opposite situation is not necessarily indicative of good health and a reflection of high motivation for counseling. Among some alcoholics flawless grooming may be only a shield or ploy to conceal continued drinking. Their attendance at group is usually a rationalization; that is, by attending they can say to themselves that even though they are drinking, they are also trying to stop.

People use more of their bodies than just their mouths to communicate. For example, Ekman and Friesen (1969) concluded that while we are talking the way we use our bodies can provide much information about our motives and give clues to our deceptions. A leader can learn about members from how they sit. For the most part, relaxed people sit casually, and anxious ones sit tensely. When the group climate becomes emotionally charged, as it often does, the leader should take time to observe members. Members' reactions are almost always reflected through facial expressions, a swinging leg, constant fidgeting, and other bodily gestures.

Participants who display immobile, impassive faces in the midst of a highly emotional session are also telling something. They may be saying that their denial and intellectualization defenses are still intact. Or they may be telling the leader and the others that they are not yet emotionally invested in the group's dynamics.

Top Dogs

A key to understanding interaction in the alcoholic group is to observe how members communicate. The Gestalt concepts of top dog and underdog (Chapter I) serve to explain these ways. Two common forms of top dogs are dictators, and analyzers.

Dictators in group, even when they speak softly, speak in terms of fiats. They perceive a black-and-white world; there are no grays, no alternatives. When the group is considering alternatives, they display their impatience by fidgeting, sighing loudly, and often becoming angry. They are happy when they are making pronouncements, and even happier when people accept the pronouncements. The biggest problems posed in group by these members is that they tend to perceive interactions as competitive, as contests they must win, if they are to maintain their dignity and self-esteem. This perception is the why of their dictatorial stance. When they dictate, they are in control; there is no competition. The spectrum of dictator types is very wide. For example, they may speak softly but with a steel edge to their tones, or loudly and gruffly. They can be articulate or inarticulate. They can be crude braggarts or be more sophisticated and brag about a relative. And there are shades and variations of all these types.

Alcoholic groups usually deal effectively with dictators. As noted, their dictatorial ways are a function of their perception. Once they learn that they do not have to compete, that there are no winners or losers in group interaction, they begin to moderate their stance and abate their fiats.

Leaders should be wary of having two dictators in the same group. They usually spot each other instantly and the group becomes a battleground. They may benefit from the ventilation, but other members may suffer. Confrontation by the group or privately by the leader is usually in order. If these methods do not work, transfer might be considered by the group and leader.

Analyzers in group generally communicate in an objective and detached way. Their remarks are usually focused although devoid of affect. They love to interpret other members' behavior and most of their talk consists of the meaning of what others say.

Analyzers do not use their analytical powers to enhance the other members but to keep them at a distance. This interpersonal stance is seen not only in their long-winded monologue but also in their tendency to sit a little apart from the group.

It is not easy to penetrate the intellectualized aura with which they surround themselves because their self-image is at the core of it. And the self-image draws upon the sometimes condescending view they take of others. Thus some analyzing alcoholic members do not just feel they are smart, but *know* they are smarter than the other members. It is to communicate that fact that they are continually analyzing.

Not all analyzers in group are condescending. Some analyze and interpret member and general group behaviors because it is the only way they know how to relate. It is the only way they ever learned.

The prime defense of the analyzer is, of course, intellectualization (Chapter II). Since emotions are not an important part of their interpersonal system, they find it difficult both to emit and to respond appropriately to them. When they try the effect is either affected or inappropriate.

Most analyzer alcoholics do want to be helped because they are very much in contact with all that goes on around them. They see other members emote, and relate warmly, angrily, happily, or sadly. They, too, want to be a part of it all. And they try to be in the only way they know—by analyzing. Unfortunately their analyses do not attract because analyses without affect are boring.

Analyzers can be helped if they are encouraged to express and focus on feelings rather than words. For example, when they are trying to self-disclose and begin to give long, tortured explanations, the leader should ask how they *"feel" now* about it. When members cry, displace, or employ any extreme behavior, the leader should direct questioning to the analyzers and, again, focus on how they feel about it.

Underdogs

Underdogs communicate as placators and weaklings.

Placators function behind a thick mask of niceness and agreeableness. The mask hides their true feelings from others and from themselves. They are so invested in the mask that they have come to believe it. Placating is a common method of communication among alcoholics. It is part of the alcoholic system of denial. It feeds the alcoholic disease.

The emotional investment in presenting the image of placator is so heavy among alcoholics that they become alienated not only from others but from themselves. They do not know what they really feel because they are first and foremost *nice,* responding positively and pleasantly to whatever the situation is for them, be it embarrassing, humiliating, or anxiety provoking.

The motivation for placating is an insatiable need to be liked and accepted. For this reason placators seldom take a stand on anything. Their fear of alienating prevents them from taking issue with anybody. Such a stand usually results in few convictions about anything. Since we are what we believe, placators usually come to feel that they are nothing.

Placators placate to gain affection and approval. They do not placate to meet others' needs or to enhance. What people think they see in placators are givers; but what they actually see are takers. Placators are takers because they are leaners. They are dependent. And their dependency fuels their feelings of guilt. Placators incorporate the most common qualities of alcoholics—denial, low self-esteem, guilt, and dependency.

Group counseling is an ideal treatment form for the placator. Placating, so common among drinking alcoholics, is phoney. This probably explains why recovering alcoholics are so sensitive to it, and why they are so good at confronting it. It is probably the drinking alcoholic's tendency toward placating that explains the recovering alcoholic's obsession with authenticity in communication.

Weaklings seem to communicate with a transparent honesty. They present themselves as weak. Their message, always delivered with much affect, often eloquently, is simple: "I am an alcoholic because I am weak."

Weaklings use honest affect and words to maneuver their listeners to respond with sympathetic words. Their objective, consciously or unconsciously, is to create the justification to continue drinking.

Like the placators weaklings have essentially surrendered to their environment and made themselves dependent on those around them. Unlike the placators, however, they do not suffer feelings of guilt because of either surrender or dependency. On the contrary they will deliver long, moving, convincing monologs on how they have been victimized into doing both. Weaklings become so adept in their delivery that often some listeners in group find themselves believing that the weaklings have a right to their feelings of victimization.

What the perceptive leader and members come to realize at some point is that no where in the weakling's message about being alcoholic because of cosmically induced weakness do they hear, "And I can change!". Once they recognize the weakling's dynamics the listeners will conclude that the long, eloquent monologs were framed in what the existentialist Sartre termed "insincere sincerity."

TRANSFERENCE

AMONG THE THREE counselors presenting their views about what qualities are necessary for an effective alcoholism group counselor, the first one indicated that the effective counselor is the one who is willing to serve as a role model. Role models are by definition subjects for identification. The prime responsibility of counselors who see themselves as role models is to create a climate in which members can identify with them; that is, they incorporate qualities, values, and behaviors of the counselor.

Identification is often the first step toward the phenomenom termed transference. Counselors who seek to serve as role models will probably facilitate identification and will inevitably promote the process of transference.

When group members go into a transference, they attach feelings onto a counselor or another member. These are feelings that they repressed long ago because of experiences with a rejecting parent figure. The rejecting parent and the counselor, even if of different sexes, unconsciously become one for the alcoholic.

The transference can be positive or it can be negative, depending on the nature of the repression effected by the parent figure. Thus if group members were too scared ever to reply with anger at being rejected and/or demeaned, they may now, in the warm accepting climate provided by the group, transfer their long repressed negative feelings onto the counselor. The object of the transference can just as easily be another member (Scheidlinger, 1984). Not uncommonly this member is one who engages in "destructive behaviors" (see Chapter III.) Favorite objects for transference are those who play the role of professional members (Rutan et al., 1984). Housekeeper types and manipulators are also frequent choices.

As noted, the transference may be positive. Group members who earlier in their lives were unable to attach feelings of love may transfer these to the counselor or another member. The sensitive, unconditionally accepting counselor is a prime target for the positive transference, as is any member who is skilled in enhancing group members' behavior. The good listener is an especially common choice by those members searching to love.

How important is the counselee transference? Psychoanalysts treat it as an inevitable phenomenon. Wolberg (1954), for example, has written that, "Sooner or later, a patient will 'transfer' past attitudes and feelings into the present relationship" (p. 677). It is because of such a view that psychoanalysts make it the focus of their counseling, whether individual or group. In none of the other rationales presented in Chapter I is such a view taken. Rogers, Perls, and Berne did not view it with the same professional interest or concern.

The eclectic position (the one here) regarding transference was expressed by its chief proponent Frederick Thorne (1950): "It is necessary for the counselor to understand it since it may be anticipated that such relationships tend to develop automatically if the counseling process reaches deep emotional levels of personality."

The eclectic view, then, is that the effective counselor knows about transference, and appreciates that it can occur. The counselor who is unaware of its existence and nature will be at a loss as to how to deal with it. To prevent that some possible symptoms of transference are indicated here.

Negative Symptoms

1. The counselor or a particular member is the constant butt of another member's hostility. (The latter is ordinarily an enhancing member.)
2. Negative comments are constantly made about counseling and/or psychology by an otherwise contributing member. (The counselor is the object here.)
3. There are periodic absences or regular tardiness.
4. Protracted periods of silence occur.
5. A member changes his or her regular seat next to a specific person to a seat away from the group.

Positive Symptoms

1. Compliments are verbalized about counseling, the group in general, and/or psychology (when the counselor is the object).
2. Body language—affectionate looks toward the transference subject and/or touching (when touching is not a typical behavior for the member)—is positive.
3. Questioning takes place concerning the subject's personal life unrelated to the group counseling.

4. A member begins to arrive regularly, and inappropriately early, who at initial meetings was at best only on time.

Treatment Alternatives

1. The counselor and/or group members may take the Rogerian or Gestalt view and simply ignore the transference dynamics and focus on the member's behavior.

2. The counselor may direct group attention to those aspects of the transference that affect the member's present life and relationships, especially in group. The focus of such direction would be upon the member's behaviors that are blocking personal progress and group process.

3. The counselor interprets and explains the nature and the why of transference in general. (Group members usually follow such explanations with intense discussion.)

4. The counselor can follow the psychoanalytic rationale and question the particular member(s) about early parent figures and ask them to relate the experiences that stand out and to discuss the relationship with such figures.

COUNTERTRANSFERENCE

Definition and Discussion

Countertransference occurs when the group counselor, or anyone else in the group who is perceived as a leader, attaches repressed feelings onto a group member or the group in general.

All group leaders are capable of a countertransference reaction. The most susceptible to it, however, will be those who lack in training, who are experiencing "burn-out," or who feel manipulated.

Whatever its reason, countertransference is a definite phenomenon. At least one researcher (Goodman, 1981) feels that such a reaction can be predictable and is a rich source of clinical data for the group, and implies that it can be used to help the group process.

The conviction here is that countertransference demeans the leader and enfeebles the group. Indeed there is research that shows that the process can damage effective confrontation and the leader's supportive techniques (Hannah, 1984). Counselors who are sensitive to their interpersonal weaknesses and who are knowledgeable about the typical symptoms of countertransference will be able to prevent it from hurting a particular member or the group in any important way.

Negative Symptoms

1. Dread about coming to session.
2. Irritability about the speech, dress, or manner of the subject member or the group.
3. Boredom or inattention during the session.
4. Lateness for sessions.
5. Inordinately slow group progress.

Positive Symptoms

1. Sexual attraction to a group member.
2. Obsession about a member.
3. Inordinate time spent grooming for a session.
4. Focus on the subject member's talk to the detriment of others.
5. Structuring of private meetings with the subject member.
6. Special treatment for the subject member.

The symptoms of countertransference, both negative and positive, would seem to be transparent. Too often they are not to the group leader in the throes of the reaction. Such a reaction is experienced by many competent and ethical counselors. Again, the best antidote is an appreciation of one's own dynamics and knowledge of the symptomatology. A series of talks with a respected colleague should prove helpful for those leaders who undergo this phenomenon.

TERMINATION

Purpose and Concerns

A member's group process ends with the termination stage. The duration of this stage varies from member to member and from group to group. Despite the variance, however, the stage should always be long enough (1) to allow members time to integrate their experience and (2) to prepare them for independence from the group.

In some alcoholism treatment centers (a minority, but still a good number), the commitment to group counseling is secondary to the pressures of client admission and space availability. In such centers group members are sometimes discharged with little or no notice to anyone but the dischargee. Leader and group find out at the next session. The effect on group cohesion is debilitating if not devastating. The prudent counselor in such a milieu will encourage the members to explore their feelings periodically about having to leave the group summarily.

In most alcoholism treatment centers, however, patients are discharged by way of staff meetings in which group leaders have a say. In this kind of setting, leaders can attend to the termination process more professionally, more effectively. Members need to know that they cannot drop out on impulse or in cavalier fashion. They need to know that an individual's termination is not just that one member's concern, but is also the business of the total group because a termination affects the total group—it alters the group personality. The leader who shares such knowledge will raise each member's self-esteem and thereby the group morale and cohesion.

Yalom (1970) has described three types of termination: (1) the unsuccessful client, (2) the successful client, and (3) the entire group.

Unsuccessful Client

Despite a leader's education about termination, there are still clients who terminate early. They drop out for a variety of reasons, including the following: they cannot handle the candor; they do not feel the group gives enough support; they are emotionally unable or are not yet ready to self-disclose to a group of alcoholic peers. After one session, and seldom more than two, such clients drop out. There are alcoholics whose personality is unsuitable for group counseling and for whom the privacy of individual counseling is a more appropriate alternative.

Sometimes clients who seem to be profiting suddenly announce they want to terminate. They may say this to the counselor privately or may tell the group in session. They usually state that they have benefited, and may even explain how. Even though the group may participate in the discussion about termination with such clients, no one seems to be satisfied. The feeling lingers with leader and group that the termination is premature. If this is so, it should be said. But the client's decision should be respected and the termination accepted.

Occasionally one termination may precipitate a number of them. This is especially true during a period of high conflict. It is important for leaders to know that such occurrences are not uncommon if a group enters the period of high conflict when group rapport and cohesion have not yet been established. Perceptive counselors can reduce, if not obviate, the dropout rate by keeping conflict at tolerable levels during these periods.

Successful Client

A telltale sign of a potential termination is when a member begins listening, responding, and assisting others when this same person had spent most of the time in group self-disclosing or discussing "me." Alcoholics who have come to this point sometimes find so much reward and therapeutic benefit in helping that they may delay their termination. They have found a therapeutic home. Moreover, they become so valuable to the group that leaders, consciously or unconsciously, support the delay. The perceptive leader will not give such support but will help move the termination process forward.

McGee and colleagues (1972) have explained that this process of termination is both comprehensive and continuous in the open group.

1. Most individuals will bring it up at the screening interview.
2. A member will express the desire or intent to terminate.
3. The group discusses the member's desire and the implications for both member and group.
4. The member will reiterate intent and confirm the decision.

5. The member attends a final meeting.
6. The group discusses termination at the subsequent meeting.
7. A new member joins the group.

What is important to note about the termination of a successful client is that the termination is really only another phase in the alcoholic's recovery process. It is an achievement, and a successful one, and should be so noted by the leader if the group does not. But it is *not* an end. Termination from group merely signals another marker on the never-ending road to recovery.

Group

The group that has specific time limits (the closed group) is not nearly as common for alcoholics as is the open group. But closed alcoholism groups do exist, for instance, the weekend marathon session.

In such groups termination time is scheduled. If the group was a successful one and cohesion was strong, the termination is invariably a loss experience. The more cohesive the group, the more intense will be the sense of loss. The prudent counselor will allow time for each member to express feelings about the group's dissolution. Leaders should also express their feelings as the termination experience invariably evokes a sense of loss in them as well (Goodyear, 1981).

SUMMARY

THE CRITERIA for selection of group members should include (1) readiness for the group, (2) ability to articulate, (3) client expectations for success, (4) client disposition to help others, and (5) sexual heterogeneity.

Rapport in group is a working relationship founded upon security and mutual help. Establishment of rapport is based on counselor competence and an explanation of roles and responsibilities. Obstacles that can block its establishment are counselor ego, an unmotivated member, and a member's negative perception of the counselor.

A setting that can facilitate group counseling has carpeted floors, curtains, pictures, and muted rather than bombastic colors. Care should be taken to provide a room of adequate size and a comfortable layout of chairs.

Communication takes place at the verbal, emotional, and behavioral levels. It is congruent when all three levels mesh. Body and emotions are inextricably interwoven. Messages can be delivered unconsciously as well as consciously. Double messages are those where words, affect, and behavior do not jibe. How one *cares* for and *uses* the body communicates much about the person. Top dogs communicate as dictators and analyzers. Underdogs communicate as placators and weaklings.

Identification is the first step toward transference, which is the attachment of feelings onto a counselor or another member. The symptoms of transference can be positive or negative.

Countertransference demeans the leader and enfeebles the group. As in transference the symptoms can be both positive and negative.

A member's group process ends in the termination stage. Termination affects the whole group because it alters the group personality. Terminations can be made by successful clients, unsuccessful clients, and entire groups. For the alcoholic termination from group merely signals another marker on the road to recovery.

REFERENCES

Bach, G. R. *Intensive Group Psychotherapy.* New York: Ronald Press, 1957.

Chaikin, A. L., Derlega, V. J., and Miller, S. J. Effects of room environment on self-disclosure in a counseling analogue. *J Couns Psychol* 23(5):479–481, 1976.

DeRivera, J. A structural theory of the emotions. *Psychol Issues* 10(4):34, 1977.

Ekman, P., and Friesen, W. V. Non-verbal leakage and clues to deception. *Psychiatry* 32:88–105, 1969.

Freud, S. *A General Introduction to Psychoanalysis.* New York: Perma Giants, 1949, pp. 25–71.

Goodman, M. Group phases and induced countertransference. *Psychother: Theory, Res Prac* 18(4):478–486, 1981.

Goodyear, R. K. Termination as a loss experience for the counselor *Personnel Guid* 59(6):347–350, 1981.

Haase, R. F. The relationship of sex and instructional set to the regulation of interpersonal interaction distance in a counseling analogue. *J Couns Psychol* 17:233–236, 1970.

Haase, R. F., and DiMattia, D. J. Spatial environments and verbal conditioning in a quasi-counseling interview. *J Couns Psychol* 23(5):414–421, 1976.

Hannah, S. Countertransference in in-patient group psychotherapy: Implications for technique. *Int Group Psychother* 34(a):257–273, 1984.

Maslow, A. H., and Mintz, N. Effect of esthetic surroundings: Initial short-term effects of three esthetic conditions upon perceiving "energy" and well-being in faces, *J Couns Psychol* 41:247–254, 1956.

McGee, T., Schuman, B., and Racusen, F. Termination in group psychotherapy *Am J Psychother* 1972.

Mintz, W. L. Effects of esthetic surroundings: Prolonged and repeated experience in a "beautiful" and ugly room. *J Psychol* 41:459–466, 1956.

Rickard, H. S. Tailored criteria of change in psychotherapy. *J Gen Psychol* 72:63–68, 1965.

Rutan, J. J., Alonsa, A., and Molin, R. Handling the absence of group leaders: To meet or not to meet. *Int J Group Psychother* 34(2):273–287, 1984.

Sadock, B., and Kaplan, H. Selection of patients in the dynamic and structural organization of the group. In H. Kaplan and B. Sadock, *The Evolution of Group Psychotherapy*. New York: Duton, 1972.

Scheidlinger, S. Psychoanalytic group psychotherapy today: An overview. *J Am Acad Psychoanal* 12(2):269–84, 1984.

Szasz, T. S. *The Myth of Mental Illness*. New York: Harper & Row, 1961, p. 302.

Thorne, F. C. Principles of personality counseling: An eclectic viewpoint *J Clin Psychol* 233, pp. 1950.

Truax, C. B., and Carkhuff, R. R. *Toward Effective Counseling and Psychotherapy: Training and Practice*. Chicago: Aldine, 1967.

Wolberg, L. R. *The Technique of Psychotherapy*. New York: Grune & Stratton, 1954, p. 677–491.

Yalom, I. *The Theory and Practice of Group Psychotherapy*. New York: Basic Books, 1970.

Chapter VI

The Group: Stages and Techniques

Counselors who understand that every member of the alcoholic group passes through a series of developmental stages will be better able to assist the member to understand not only personal behaviors and reactions but what is happening generally, and perhpas even why. To be effective counselors need to understand (1) the characteristics of these stages, (2) the contemporary behaviors and defenses associated with each stage, (3) the communication style typical of a stage, and (4) the technique they need to employ to deal effectively with each stage. In this chapter the five stages through which a member passes in the *open group* will be examined.

It is important to note that the stages as analyzed and outlined here ordinarily do not occur in a numerical, predetermined order. The next sequence that follows was adopted purely to present an orderly and thorough explanation. The dynamics explained all take place, but in a haphazard, human fashion. Thus members will frequently progress from the first stage to the second and then regress to the first. Sometimes they seem to move through the first two stages at the initial session and at the next session to regress to the first; then stay there for a dozen sessions! The truth is that stages do not end sharply but rather blend and merge into one another. For this reason it is usually very difficult to determine where a member is. The exception is when the member has reached the fifth stage—termination.

How long it takes to pass from the first through the fifth stage varies with the member. Chief factors in the variance seem to be motivation to achieve sobriety and ability to adapt to the group. This latter factor seems to be most affected by how articulate the member is.

Stage one is the acclimation stage. It is characterized by newness, insecurity, member testing, and fumbling methods of communication. The most effective techniques counselors can employ at this stage are questioning, reiterating, reflecting, recapitulating, and listening.

A feeling of place and position in the group together with a feeling of rapport characterize stage two. Communication is at all levels—verbal, emotional, and behavioral—but is not often congruent. The counselor's techniques include self-disclosing and clarifying as well as those of stage one.

Conflict dominates the third stage. Transferences are in full bloom. There is a beginning awareness that the individual is responsible for his or her own alcoholism. The prime counselor technique is confrontation, with probing a close second.

In the fourth stage the members work hard disclosing, reacting, and finding out about themselves. Feelings and personal meanings are freely described and accepted with facility. Admissions of personal responsibility are common—the alcoholic sense of victimization may decline sharply. The member begins to find much reward in helping others. All the techniques used in the first three stages are used here.

The fifth stage is concerned with termination. Denial about self and alcohol has evaporated as members become aware that they do not need the group. They look and feel comfortable with themselves. Their newly found sense of emotional integration is such that they are willing to take risks being themselves, being accepted or rejected by others.

STAGE ONE—ACCLIMATION

ACCLIMATION TO A GROUP is anxiety provoking for anybody. It is especially so for the alcoholic. The constant, latent suspicions and fears with which the typical new member is beset invariably become more acute with the prospect of a new experience, particularly one that obligates interaction with a number of people. Upon entry into group, the acute discomfort felt, combined with the usual weak alcoholic controls, invariably affects the alcoholic personality negatively.

The advent of a new personality will, of course, alter the group personality. The group, like the member, will enter a period of discomfort. Leaders share in this discomfort. Counselors always feel some anxiety with a new entry. Such feelings are part of their identification with the group. Leaders are concerned with both the quality of impact that the new person will make and the group's reception. If they are not, they are not prepared to deal with the new member.

A leader's concern here is to help the new member feel at home as quickly as possible. The sooner the member does this, the sooner exaggerated and testing behaviors will be dropped and the sooner the group's feelings of discomfort will evaporate. When the feelings of discomfort have evaporated, the group will have its new personality.

More often than not, the ongoing open group does this with little or no leader guidance. Members who are in the advanced stages of the process are especially sensitive and willing to help new members become acclimated. The leader can sense that this is happening when testing behaviors decline and behaviors become more sedate.

In stage one the new member's system of communication is concerned with externals. There is a general unwillingness to self-disclose or to communicate the self in any meaningful way. Feelings are not usually recognized accurately. Often the new member's anxiety and lack of congruence are reflected in an inordinate number of contradictory statements.

Techniques

Behaviors and Defenses

The anxiety engendered by entry into group may bring out a new member's most eccentric behaviors or, at best, usual behaviors but in exaggerated form. The quiet member may become mute, the clown appear to be positively hypomanic, the professional types boorish, or the antagonist to be carrying a log rather than a chip.

Such behaviors may be the only ones that the new member knows to communicate personal uneasiness. They may also be the ways the member has learned to test others: "How much will they take before they all reject me?" Such a rationale is common among alcoholics.

Most of the behaviors exhibited in this stage are those defined as "destructive" (see Chapter III). The techniques that deal most effectively with these are designed to assist individuals to focus on what they are doing and feeling. More specifically they are techniques that set the stage for the mitigation and redirection of the defenses that both feed and protect these behaviors.

At this stage the defenses most commonly used for the support of the denial defense are displacement, fantasy, projection, rationalization, intellectualization, and regression. The best way to deal with these defenses at this stage is not to feed them. However, they should not be challenged either because to do so might alienate the new member, and might even cause dropping out.

The techniques used in this stage are:

1. Questioning.
2. Reiterating.
3. Reflecting.
4. Recapitulating.
5. Listening.

Questioning

Questioning, especially in stage one, should be done with caution. The purpose by definition is to elicit information. The problem is that the new members might feel that the information is too private to share with people whom they still consider strangers. Questions, whether by the leader or a peer, often fuel their suspicions and strengthen the projection defense. A major problem with questioning new members is that it might alienate them rather than facilitate closeness.

In group questions sometimes set off more questions. Person A's question triggers person B's question, which in turn triggers person C's question. If the leader is not careful to prevent such a barrage, the new member may begin to feel like a hostile witness, if not the defendant in a courtroom spectacle.

Questions at best can beget answers. They do not ordinarily precipitate self-disclosure, voluntary self-expression, or self-examination.

The major drawback to questioning is probably the fact that it is primarily an intellectual and not an emotional process. Intellectualized exchanges can be helpful in group, but when they occur without emotional appreciation, their value is debatable. In fact such exchanges may abet the new member's intellectualization defense.

Despite these drawbacks, questioning can be valuable if done properly. At the new member's initial meeting, questions should always be gentle in tone and friendly, and, if possible, should be in response to the new member's comments. If the new member has not yet spoken, then the questions should be derived from the comments the leader made when introducing the newcomer. If the group is able to adhere to this idea, it will avoid touching on any areas with which the new member is not yet ready to deal.

The group members can communicate that they do not want to touch on any emotional sore spots by asking open-ended questions rather than questions that require a several-word response. One question should not be followed by another until the new member has had ample opportunity to respond to the first.

Neither the new member's denial defense nor any of its supporting defenses should be challenged with questions during stage one. Such a challenge would threaten the member unnecessarily and might lead to alienation, if not premature termination.

Reiterating

This technique is derived from the Rogerian rationale for the encounter group. It is primarily the leader's technique. This author has noticed that it is used by members who are in the advanced stages and professional-type members in particular.

As the term indicates, reiterating is a literal restatement of what a member has said. The words tell the new member that his or her message has been received; their effect should indicate that they are accepted.

Reiterating is a particularly good technique for this stage because the reiterator is immediately cast into the role of an accepting person, someone each new member is looking for. Reiterators are invariably the people to whom new members initially address their comments.

The special merit of stage one lies in what it does *not* do. It does not threaten because it is nonconfrontative. Reiterating cannot raise any anxieties or fears or inadvertently offend. The worst interpretation that the most suspicious new alcoholic member can assign a reiterative comment is that it is neutral.

Finally, a note of caution about reiteration. There is a risk in using it too frequently as the user, whether leader or member, may begin to sound a little like "Little Sir or Lady Echo."

Reflecting Feeling

In reflecting feeling a counselor or a participant mirrors the emotion expressed by a group member. Reflecting feeling is a technique that expresses empathy. When feelings are reflected effectively, the communication is, "I see as you see and I appreciate the reality you perceive." Such a communication invariably mitigates the alcoholic sense of isolation.

Appropriate at all stages, it is eminently so at a later session of a member's first stage. When a leader or participants reflect a first-stage member's feelings, they address themselves to that member's emotion, not to intellectual content. As in reiteration, then, there is no confrontative-like challenge, and therefore little chance of alienating the member. Indeed with reflecting there are added bonuses. The confusion that members feel at this stage is ameliorated because their feelings are shared and with this they are perceived and understood more clearly. In short they are crystallized. The sense of sharing and crystallized understanding help to move the client to the second stage.

Highlen and Baccus (1977) studied the effects of counselor reflection of feeling on 40 female subjects. These researchers found that this technique was very effective in both eliciting and clarifying emotion when it was self-referenced.

In reflecting feelings certain technical points should be kept in mind. The language that the leader uses should be language that fits the member's style of interaction. It is language the leader knows the member uses and with which he or she feels comfortable. The easiest way to do this is to use the words that the member used. The author varies words only to avoid sounding like a parrot.

Another point to be remembered about reflecting is timing. Reflecting should be done immediately after a member's feelings are expressed.

If leaders let extraneous material intervene between the member's expression and the reflecting, the reflecting will be minimized, if not missed.

Finally, although words need not and probably should not be the same, the reflecting emotion should, as far as possible, be identical. If it is not, the affective message to the member should be that that was precisely the intention. This is best accomplished by the leader's body language, especially facial expressions, and the sincerity of the leader's tone.

Recapitulating

Members at the first stage often engage in long, unfocused monologs. The particular reasons for this vary but generally they are caused by insecurity, confusion, or perhaps a need to test the leader and the group: "How much you take from me shows me how much you love me."

Sometimes these long monologs are founded in the new member's method of interaction. If nothing else, they establish distance, a common method among alcoholics. Thus the new member might be telling the group, "I'm here but I don't want to get close to anybody—yet." The "yet," of course, is what the leader must interpret. The real message of the monolog might be that it is only a transitional phenomenon until the member feels more comfortable, or it might be that it is a habitual method of relating. Perceptive leaders will be able to tell this soon enough. Their recapitulating can help the group better understand the meaning of the member's unfocused monologs.

When leaders recapitulate they respond to the monolog with a focused, succinct synopsis. Recapitulating is primarily an intellectual mode of communication. As far as possible, the idioms and key words used should be the ones used in the monolog.

When the leader or group members recapitulate, they communicate that they are listening and there are several benefits to such communication.

1. The new member's insecurity, confusion, and need to test are all mitigated.
2. The new member is helped to focus thoughts and adhere to a theme.
3. The leader and group are reinforced in their own understanding.

Upon this foundation rapport is promoted and the new member is helped toward the second stage.

Listening

In Chapter III listening was listed as one of the enhancing behaviors. The discussion dealt with the fact that alcoholics generally have never learned how to listen, but that the leader needs to promote it if members are to progress toward health. The discussion here will focus on how the leader can engender a climate conducive to listening.

More than two decades ago, Patterson (1963) wrote that listening is "the most basic, most universal, most important technique in counseling and psychotherapy." The conviction here is that it remains so. It has to. No group can function if the leader and members do not listen to each other. Rapport, cohesion, sharing, and personal growth—in short, the very purpose of the group, the therapeutic process—cannot proceed without listeners.

Listening is not easy. Nobody is a born listener. It is a learned skill and in general alcoholics never learned it. For whatever reason they were always too turned in on themselves to do so. Most show this during the first stage of counseling by how they relate to each other. Irrelevant questions, interruptions, unasked-for advice, and whispered side conversations are indicative. Such behaviors reflect and can only reinforce the basic perception and understanding that alcoholics have—that nobody really listens.

To counter such a perception, the effective leader will demonstrate good listening skills. To do that the leader must understand that there are two important aspects to listening: (1) phasis and (2) strepitus (Westcott, 1966).

Phasis refers to the feelings, tones, and sounds on which words ride. The counselor who is as sensitive to these as to the member's verbal content will communicate infinitely better than the one who focuses on words only. Such a counselor will be telling the new member that "we want to get close." Counselors who are sensitive to phasis should acknowledge a member's affect. "The way you punctuated those last couple of sentences with a chuckle tells us that you're not all that mad, Jack. Am I right?"

Strepitus refers to the sounds generated by another person—foot tapping, finger drumming, making a chair creak because of constant shifting. Westcott explained that these sounds are as much a part of an individual's system of communication as are the words and voice tones. What they reflect particularly are the person's anxieties. To respond to them is to respond to the whole person and to communicate a full acceptance. If the leader feels there is a budding rapport between a new member and the group, such a communication can be made facetiously. "John, that foot routine would have done Fred Astaire proud. Sitting down yet!" The point is that comments such as these communicate that leader and group are attuned to all of the new member, not just to particular aspects of the person.

It is not enough just to listen to the new member, but the *motivation* to do so must also be communicated. In doing so the leader will be enhancing the newcomer and will be telling all the members that listening is of paramount concern. (Implied in such a message is that they should learn to do so.) The following practical techniques not only will help achieve both purposes, but will also teach the group how to listen.

1. Body language is basic to good listening. How the leader *sits* tells the member how much the former wants to listen. How leaders sit is in part a function of personality. Generally speaking, casual people sit casually, and formal people sit formally. The issue is comfort and a counselor who is comfortable will communicate that fact, will set the tone for more comfortable interaction.

Counselors should position themselves so that they can observe and be observed by every member. Their constant communication should be that the talking member is the focal point of attention and interest.

2. Leaders should structure their sessions so there are *no interruptions*. It should be made clear to other staff and secretaries that they are incommunicado while counseling the group. Except for the most extreme emergencies, the policy should be that, for both leader and group members, all messages can wait. The "Do Not Disturb" sign on the closed door is appropriate. Such procedures communicate to the new member that during the scheduled session the group is the focus of the leader's full attention.

3. Effective listeners are those who have learned to *insulate themselves from distracting* thoughts. Frequently leaders will come to a session with a nagging concern, a personal worry. If they are to communicate that

they are listening, they will need to learn to compartmentalize such thoughts. (These ideas were dealt with more fully in Chapter V. A rereading at this point might prove helpful.)

4. Leaders need to know those *words* or topics that precipitate internal revulsion. For example, there are a host of racial slurs that group members may use to justify personal hatreds and biases. Leaders should know which of them trigger negative reactions that they cannot conceal, which of them lower their esteem of the member who uses them. If the leaders do not have a thorough self-knowledge about their own reactions to prejudice, they will have trouble listening and communicating generally. The author's view is that this topic needs to be one of those that leaders compartmentalize. However strong one's conscience about human equality, group counseling of the alcoholic is simply not the forum in which to debate or try to convince a member of the group about the moral wrong of ethnic, religious, or sexual prejudice. Members are there because of their addiction, not to work through their biases. Even though biases are an aspect of their authoritarianism, they should not be made a focal point of discussion. Such topics invariably resurrect intense feelings. This author's experience is that resurrections accomplish little to ameliorate the prejudice, and nothing at all to promote maintenance of sobriety.

5. The *questions* asked of new members will communicate how well they are being listened to. Questions should be in response to a new member's comments and should not introduce new topics.

STAGE TWO—RAPPORT AND COHESION

AT STAGE TWO the new members' feelings of threat, although extant, have begun to dissipate. They are beginning to feel accepted and, in turn, to accept the group. An honest sense of trust has begun to form. They feel thay have both place and position in the group. In a real sense, they feel they have found an emotional shelter where they can do what they have never done—get to know themselves. At this stage new members want to be a part of the group.

Despite this new identity with the group, most new members are still not ready to self-disclose, at least not at the beginning of this stage. They are not ready because they have not yet learned how.

New members at this stage begin to acknowledge that they have important personal problems. The problems, however, are still perceived for the most part as being external rather than internal. The switch to internal occurs in this stage.

During this stage members step up descriptions of their feelings and personal meanings. But it is important to note that such descriptions and meanings are concerned with events of long ago. In any case there is a much freer flow of expression at this stage. Toward the end of this stage, some new members begin to make minor self-disclosures about the pain they are currently experiencing. Before the end of this stage, most members begin to recognize that the problems lie within rather than without. There is a move toward acceptance of one's own self.

Stage two may best be recognized as a learning stage. It is here that members make their first fumbling attempts to learn who they are, why they came from where they did, and, most important, where it is that they are going.

Techniques

Behavior and Defenses

Despite the rapport and cohesion that characterize this stage, many members occasionally regress to the destructive behaviors they engaged in at the first stage. Thus a member might be absent, lapse into hostile silences, give vent to antagonisms, and so forth. The reasons for this are simple. Old ways die hard. But it is only if these regressions intrude on the group, or the member seems to be finding greater reward in them, or the newer, enhancing behaviors are not becoming more dominant, that the leader should engage in confrontation.

In most instances these regressions are sporadic and short lived. The new spirit of camaraderie with which the member comes to identify invariably results in identification also with the enhancing behaviors (see Chapter III) displayed by the other members. The self-disclosing of others, their apparent trust, as well as kindly feedback, lead the new member to attempt the same.

At this stage the denial defense is weaker but still in evidence. Its supporting defenses such as displacement, fantasy, projection, rationalization, intellectualization, and regression are in apparent decline. At this stage the member's need to deny who they are or their alcoholism is not nearly as acute as it was at stage one.

The prudent leader will recognize that a member at the second stage is a member who can still be a dropout. For this reason the techniques employed, like those of the first stage, should not challenge, but also should not reward, destructive behaviors. They should only increase movement toward the third stage. This can be done by solidifying the member's identification with the group and helping him or her find reward in the enhancing behavior. As noted, this is still very much a learning stage.

In addition to all of the techniques used in stage one, the most effective techniques here are self-disclosure (see Chapter III) and clarification.

Self-disclosure

When leaders self-disclose they are telling new members that they want to get close and that it is alright to get close. But they are telling them more. They are saying that candor and authenticity are held in esteem in group and that pretensions have no place.

A leader's self-disclosure should be like any self-disclosure—forthright, appropriately affective, and completely honest. If the leader is a recovering alcoholic, to share that is appropriate. As noted before there is little disclosure that can facilitate member rapport with the group faster than that bit of information. The telling of that fact, together with complementary incidents that can communicate the pain that the leader went through, can only strengthen the member's identification with the group.

Self-disclosures by the leader should always be founded in astuteness. Thus they should always be relevant to the group discussion and be designed to enhance rapport and cohesiveness. In no case should the leader's disclosures be tinged with braggadocio or one-up-manship. Such disclosures never enhance, can demean, and can be painfully embarrassing.

Clarification

When leaders clarify they update and throw light on a group discussion just finished. They pick out the central theme of a discussion or interaction and expand upon it. Clarifying is a kind of first cousin to feedback. When leaders clarify they explain what is going on in group. This is an important technique because too often the intellectualizers in group play semantic games, creating the opportunity for the group to get lost in trivial side discussions.

For those members at stage two who still operate with a cynical rationale, what a clarifying leader communicates is that the group is not just a "bull" session but is concerned, and vitally, with concrete progress. For the new member who continues to hide behind long, ruminating, unfocused monologs, clarifying leaders communicate that they care and are listening. "What I got out of what you just said John is. . . ." Not incidentally, leaders who clarify also help the members whose thinking is still confused and irrelevant to become more focused.

Clarifying is a valuable technique not only for the member at stage two, but also for the whole group. It is especially appropriate at the end of a session to elucidate a theme of the hour. "Now, what each of us has said one way or another is that Alice should hold off for at least two more sessions before she terminates." It is most appropriate at the end of a short but heated group interaction to help members reflect on the feelings expressed. It is also apt to act at the beginning of a session as a springboard or a bridge to help the group better understand the theme of the last session so that members may determine if they want to continue exploring in the same vein.

STAGE THREE—CONFLICT

THE BEST WAY to understand stage three is to see it as the stage where the member is highly motivated to search for his or her own self. It is a search for identity. In stage two the search was a fumbling one, inhibited by fear and self-doubt. At this stage members feel they can emotionally afford to air their conflicts and direct their energy to finding out who they really are.

This is the stage where a member's identification with another member or the leader may move into a full-blown transference. By venting feelings onto another, the member hopes to develop a satisfying relationship—something never experienced before.

It is when members are at this stage, too, that leaders might find themselves in the throes of a countertransference. The reason for this is that it is at stage three that members exhibit the extreme behaviors. It is these behaviors that can most easily facilitate countertransferences.

At this stage feelings and personal meanings are described as *now* feelings and not just those of long ago. For the first time, alcoholics begin to admit to personal responsibility for their behavior. Their victimization syndrome evaporates. At this stage members may leave the group on an emotional "high." They have moments when they feel as though they are "experiencing" life for the first time. They give and receive affect appropriately and easily.

TECHNIQUES

Behaviors and Defenses

In stage three, destructive behaviors abate rapidly and enhancing behaviors increase in both type and frequency. Sometimes the conflict between the two becomes dramatically evident in the extreme behaviors—weeping, assaulting, and seducing.

The decrease in the destructive behaviors is based on the diminished threat felt. That the clown type usually becomes more sophisticated and gentle, the professional type does not volunteer professionalism but plays the role of a senior diplomat and waits for members to ask for an opinion, and the silent type begins to interact are examples of the movement toward enhancing behavior. The destructive behavior most in evidence at this stage is antagonism. Anger built up over the years does not dissipate easily or rapidly. Alcoholics hold on to it. It is almost as if they feel there will be a void if they give it up. They continue to displace. Indeed one sometimes has the impression that it is actually increasing, but it is not. The intensity may be more acute but at this stage the displacements, while very real and disturbing, can be validly seen as reactions to the stress of a weakening denial defense and a changing disposition. Nowhere is this change seen more clearly than in the member's self-disclosing, in the sudden interest in receiving others' feedback, and in the new interest in giving it and in helping others.

Behaviors such as these, of course, mean that the individuals are redirecting their energy and defenses. Sublimation usually is a function of redirected energy. At this stage it begins to become prime in the interpersonal method. The supporting defenses for sublimation are usually redirected ones; that is, where the members used intellectualization to professionalize and bore, they may now explain and analyze the feedback they deliver.

Now that the member is both identified and involved in the group, the most effective techniques that can be used are those that challenge. These are confronting and probing.

Confronting

The technique that is indispensable at this stage is confronting. According to Cohen (1981) the confronting technique can serve effectively as a rationale throughout the whole process. Whether or not this technique can do so is debatable. What is not debatable is that with alcoholics there comes a point in group process when it is necessary.

It is important that the leader recognize that this technique, even when couched in the gentlest and kindest tones, can still be viewed as harsh and threatening. Accordingly leaders should be fully confident that the members recognize that the confronting remarks come from an interested, caring orientation. "We all have our bad days, Alice. Seems like you're not having your best one today. Think you can tell us why?"

Confronting effectively requires three competencies: (1) the ability to pick the proper affective moment, (2) the ability to discern that the members can handle it, and (3) the ability to see that the member can profit from it.

When members confront each other without these competencies, it muddles and blocks group progress. If the leader is not able in these three areas, the effect on the members confronted, and on the group as a whole, can be debilitating; for instance, members sympathetic to the one confronted will form an alliance against the leader, now a "bad guy."

Confronting an alcoholic member is always risky. Nevertheless the merits of this technique continue to be worth the risk.

1. It attacks the deadly and infectious aspects of the member's disease.
2. It addresses the last vestiges of the denial defense.
3. It brings the alcoholic face to face with the need to take responsibility.
4. It helps alcoholics to see that they do in fact have choices.
5. It helps prepare them for termination and ultimate independence from the group.

When the leader confronts the alcoholic member, the message implied should be, even in the most oblique kind of remark or question, "Booze can kill you and everybody associated with you."

At this stage the member's denial of his or her alcoholism is weak. Confronting at this point further breaks down the denial, and may even alleviate it entirely.

Confronting tells members that they are like everybody else in this world, and that if they are ever going to be mature, they need to be accountable for their behavior. The confronting message is, "You simply can no longer afford to be a baby."

Confronting tells the group member that there are alternatives in life. One does not have to submit to a demeaning, destructive enabler. One can choose to run one's own life. Divorce or living elsewhere are always viable alternatives.

It is only if they are confronted and made to reflect upon the cruel reality of their past lives that alcoholics can appreciate where they have been. The conviction here is that that kind of cathartic experience can help them to formulate plans and resolutions to achieve some measure of fulfillment in their future lives.

Probing

When the leader probes, members are helped to search more deeply into themselves, and more particularly into their motives. Probing is an especially effective and appropriate technique for alcoholics because it addresses one of their major deficiencies, namely, their unwillingness to take responsibility for their behavior. When leaders probe they motivate members to examine the whys of their behavior.

Most people are a little afraid to explore such whys. Alcoholics seem to labor under a constant latent terror that if they were to explore whys, they might find valid reasons to shoot themselves at sunrise.

Probing is an investigative technique. Neither counselor nor member can know precisely where probes will lead. To be productive, then, the counselor needs to have some appreciation of what the members' especially sensitive spots are. Moreover, all probes should have a tentative quality so that a member can maneuver and choose in responding. Probes should not corner or manipulate a member into a response, but should be designed to encourage the member to self-explore.

Member: "I know I'm mad. I'm mad all the time and I don't know why."

Leader: "You're mad all the time. Can you identify the times when it seems the worst?"

Probes framed in such a way give the members a feeling of space, encourage them to explore and at the same time tell them that the choice to share or not to share is theirs. The purpose of probing is to meet the individual member's needs, not those of the leader.

STAGE FOUR—WORK

AT THIS STAGE the member begins to perceive self and others more realistically and more clearly. Interaction with others in the group becomes increasingly rewarding.

Feelings are freely expressed and are accepted easily. Denial about self and behavior, especially as it relates to alcohol, is discussed and emotionally appreciated. Contradictions in past and current behavior are recognized and admitted. The member expresses in various ways the desire to be "the real me" and begins to question the values, attitudes, and behaviors that led to alcoholism. Exploration of these inevitably leads to a sense of responsibility for one's life and behavior.

Those members who are in a transference or countertransference usually work toward its resolution and emerge with a stronger ego. These are the members in whom the group does indeed effect personality changes.

In the initial sessions of this stage, any destructive behaviors in evidence are carryovers from the preceding stages but are considerably mellowed. By the end of the stage, they have greatly evaporated. The enhancing behaviors begun in earlier stages are reinforced and increased.

In general the member's interactions are characterized by helping others (this is true even for those in the process of resolving a transference or countertransference.)

While members make use of the whole kaleidoscope of defenses available, the one most in evidence is, as in the preceding stage, sublimation.

STAGE FIVE—TERMINATION

THE MEMBERS who reach the termination stage feel and look comfortable. Their system of communication is congruent, inconsistencies are minimal. These members, even though actively participatory, invariably have also developed a strong introspective bent.

The persons who reach this stage accept themselves fully. Such acceptance is the reason they become accepting and tolerant of others. And such acceptance, of course, removes the need to deny.

The members who terminate through the group process have reached that point in their growth where they feel they can *risk*. They can risk leaving the group because they feel they can risk being themselves—can risk being hurt, being rejected, and being accepted.

SUMMARY

THE FIVE STAGES of the group process do not ordinarily occur in a neat, predetermined order. More commonly group members pass through them in a haphazard fashion.

Stage one is the acclimation stage. It is characterized by the member's sense of newness, insecurity, testing of the group and leader, and fumbling methods of communication. The techniques recommended in this stage are questioning, reiterating, reflecting, recapitulating, and listening.

Stage two is distinguished by the member's sense of rapport, place, and position in the group. Communication is at all levels but is not often congruent. Self-disclosing and clarifying are prime techniques.

Stage three is dominated by conflict. Transferences are in full bloom. The member's sense of responsibility begins to bud. Prime techniques at this stage include both confrontation and probing.

Stage four is the stage where members work hard finding out about themselves. Interaction with others in the group becomes increasingly rewarding. Feelings are freely expressed and accepted. Transferences and countertransferences are ordinarily resolved. The prime defense is sublimation.

Stage five is the termination stage. Members feel and look comfortable. Communication is congruent. Members at this stage accept themselves fully. They now feel they can risk being themselves.

REFERENCES

Cohen, A. I. Confrontation analysis in groups: Goals of treatment. *Psychother: Theory, Res Pract* 4:441–456, 1981.

Highlen, P. S., and Baccus, G. K. Effect of feeling and probe on client self-referenced affect *J Couns Psychol* 24(5):440–443, 1977.

Patterson, C. N. *Counseling and Psychotherapy: Theory and Practice.* New York: Harper & Row, 1959, p. 168.

Westcott, R. Introducing coenetics. *Am Schol* 35: 342–356, 1966.

Chapter VII

Group Activities

Not every alcoholism group needs to become involved in activities. Indeed, many do not. The personality of a given group may be such that there never seems to be enough time to address and deal with its basic and integral issues. Activities and exercise seem to be extraneous, if not irrelevant to such a group.

There are other groups that can profit a great deal from planned and designed activities. Such activities center around the central issues of the alcoholism group—listening and communication.

CRITERIA

Purpose

This criterion takes precedence over all others. Activities should be introduced only if they have a definite objective and one that responds to member needs. The popularity or fashionableness of an activity is simply not a valid criterion for its introduction into group. What goal does the leader hope to attain? What member or group needs will be met? The competent leader should be able to answer both these questions before an activity is introduced.

Leader Expertise

How receptive the group is to an activity will be influenced by the leader's enthusiasm and confidence about its value. This enthusiasm and confidence should be a function of the leader's experience with the activity. Leaders should not choose an activity on the basis of reading or hearsay. They should have had personal contact with it, if not in their professional role of leader, then as a coleader or student leader, or as members themselves. To choose an activity without having participated in it can promote failure of that activity and can in turn result in a lowered member confidence in the leader's competence.

Appropriateness

The activity should be one with which members are comfortable. It should take into account the age of the group members. For example, a group of children of alcoholics might prefer using dolls to explore their feelings rather than role playing. An adult group would probably prefer role playing. In short, the activity chosen should respond to the interests of the group. Activities that do not spark interest or that constrain or embarrass will weaken group rapport, and even alienate members.

Maximum Sharing

The activity selected should always promote maximum sharing by all members. Accordingly the experiential, intellectual, and emotional levels of all group members need to be weighed.

An activity that requires all members to self-disclose and/or to give feedback is not appropriate if a new member is present. Such an activity, to be effective, necessitates a maximum of familiarity with the group.

The intellectual competence of the members also needs to be taken into account when a leader is considering an activity that requires demanding verbal skills.

Finally, if a member is still in the recovery stages of an acute loss or neurotic episode, the prudent leader would do well not to choose activities that might effect extreme behavior in any of the members.

Retention of Choice

All members must have the right to choose whether or not to participate in an activity. If they do not feel they have the choice, then the group's therapeutic value is lost. The therapeutic value of group lies in the motivation of the members to participate. This motivation is a function of the members' internal needs. It is not a function of external pressure by the leader.

The purpose of the activity chosen is to increase the alcoholic members' sense of independence and personal choice. Such a sense can only enhance them. The diminuition of this sense compounds their sense of being controlled, manipulated, and victimized. These, of course, are the prime feelings with which alcoholics enter the group. Should they be reinforced, the group has lost all value for them.

Learning and Application

An activity has special meaning for participants when they learn from it and can apply the meaning to their lives. The member who learns to improve listening skills, who learns how and when to self-disclose, will function better not only in group, but outside of it as well. An activity that accomplishes this purpose has met the most important criterion of all.

LISTENING ACTIVITIES

MEMBERS WHO LEARN how to reiterate, reflect, probe, and question the thoughts and feelings of another will be members who learn to listen effectively.

Have a member pair off with another, someone whom they do not know well. This can be done easily enough if the leader does the pairing. Make sure that each pair has enough space so that it does not interfere with another pair.

Reiterating and Reflecting

1. Have one member make a statement about himself or herself. The statement should be made in a flat tone, be unemotional, and contain a dozen or so words. The member's partner then *must reiterate the statement verbatim.* If there is even a one-word alteration in the reiteration, then the first person repeats the statement until it is reiterated exactly. Each person has to reiterate three statements precisely.

2. Have one of the paired members make a personal statement of a dozen or so words but this time there should be a strongly affective quality in the tone. The reiteration and reflection must satisfy the speaker. Continue the exercise until both members have responded successfully three times.

3. Have the pairs talk for 15 minutes on an aspect of alcoholism upon which they can mutually agree. The rule they must follow is that once one of them has said anything, the other may not add a word until the first person judges that his or her comments have been reiterated and reflected satisfactorily.

The purpose of these exercises is to help the members focus on what the other person is saying rather than on what one wants to say. This approach is especially valuable in helping members to see how easy it is to let one's own feelings and thoughts interfere with listening.

Questioning

Have one member of a pair ask the other a personal question about how alcohol has affected his or her life.

If possible, the question should relate to an aspect of personal history that the questioned member has at best only touched on in group and that the questioner feels has been avoided—an emotional sore spot. The sore spot, however, is not really rubbed because the one questioned is not to answer the question but to respond with, "I think what you're asking me is . . . ," explaining the perceived purpose and significance of the question. If this response is confirmed by the questioner, then the second person asks a personal question. Each person gets three confirmations as to what they perceive to be the intent of the question.

What members learn in this exercise is that there can be differences in the understanding of the intention and meaning of a question between the questioner and the one questioned. There is even more value for alcoholics in this exercise as the constant, latent paranoia with which they are beset is faced squarely and honestly.

Probing

One member of a pair is asked to make a personal statement about how alcohol has affected thinking, emotional reactions, personality, and/or life in general. The partner's response is a probe. "You are telling me that . . . or what I'm hearing is that . . . Is that right?" The addition to these by the partner is a statement about what the personal statement means. The first member then affirms or negates the accuracy of the probe. Each member has to obtain three affirmations to complete the exercise.

The exercise tells both partners how really difficult it is to probe accurately, to fathom the feelings, thoughts, and general experience of another person.

COMMUNICATION ACTIVITIES

The activities presented in the following describe the three levels through which group members usually pass. These are breaking the ice, learning and maintaining, and termination.

Level One—Breaking the Ice

1. *Name tags.* Have members prepare name tags with four descriptive words, two ending in *able* and two in *ing.* An example might be John Jones: lovable, laudable, helping, fascinating. Have members introduce themselves explaining why they have chosen their adjectives. Following the introductions, let members mill around talking for five to ten min-

utes. Reconvene the group and let members add additional "ing" and "able" words to describe themselves and others.

This is an especially effective exercise for the initial meeting of a closed group.

2. *Rounds.* Have the group make rounds. It begins with the leader stating his or her name. The next member repeats it and gives his or her own name. It continues with each member introducing him or herself and repeating the name of all the preceding members until everyone learns the name of each member. Once this is accomplished, have each person add a current hobby or interest such as, "Like I said, I'm John Jones and I used to be nuts about beer but now I'm nuts about jigsaw puzzles." Repeat the process until each person can identify each other not only by name, but also by interests.

This also is effective with the closed group at the initial session.

3. *Self-description.* In this exercise members are asked to describe themselves. Instructions call for them to use only the third person in their description. Thus they can be asked to describe themselves as the person they would most like to be (their ideal) or as their own best friend. The purpose of this exercise is to help the more inhibited and introverted members (the new ones especially) to self-disclose. The use of the third person alleviates the anxiety of self-disclosure and gives each group member an insight into the dynamics of the member describing and relating. When done, the relating member can be asked about the "mythical ideal or best friend" in the third person.

How well this exercise is carried out will depend on how effectively leaders guide their group. They should studiously remind members to keep their questions of each other in the third person. A most effective way to ensure success of this activity is for the leader to start it by acting as a role model for the self-disclosure technique.

Level Two—Learning and Maintaining

An activity that strongly encourages communication is *role playing.* It is an activity that enlightens those who play and those who observe. When members role-play, they act the part of another person as they perceive that person would act in a given situation. Effective role players are those who can assume and act out the behavior of another group member. Roles played with honesty and sincerity provide the role players with a look into the perceptual frames of reference of the member whose role they are playing. It gives the member whose behavior is being role-played a rare opportunity to see how he or she is viewed by others. Members are usually surprised to find out how well they can act out another member's speech and behavior. Sometimes players identify with the role so well that they feel they are actually experiencing the feelings of the one whom they are playing.

In the alcoholic group, certain of the member types can provide ideal models for role players. Among these are the clown, the housekeeper, the professional member, and the manipulator. The performance by other members invariably provides these types with insight into their behavior, and the effect is usually a decline in its more destructive aspects. The greatest benefit from this activity for both member and group seems to accrue when a member is at the third and fourth stages of the group.

Role playing can be carried out in a variety of ways.

1. Empty chair.
2. Role reversal.
3. Role substitution.
4. Ego crutch.

The *empty chair* technique was first explained by the Gestaltist, Fritz Perls. Members, at the request of the leader, put an aspect of their personality into an empty chair and talk to it. The aspects might be an overscrupulous conscience, a condescending attitude, or an excessive timidity. By putting the aspect of themselves into the chair, the participants are able to experience *being* that aspect and not just talking about it.

Role reversal was also first introduced by Perls. Two members are asked to sit in the center of the group and each to play the other person.

Especially appropriate for such casting are a silent and an antagonistic member. The drama of the reversal can be heightened further if the leader at midpoint interrupts them and asks them to switch roles, and relate to each other as themselves. A switch back to the reverse roles should be made one more time. The rationale for this technique is that by playing the role of a person who is a direct opposite, one can touch upon a new part of oneself, a part that has been previously denied.

A variation of the role-reversal technique is *role substitution.* In this activity members can gain insight into how they are perceived by others by watching a two- or three-member skit in which they are portrayed as the main character. Clown types, housekeepers, and professional members particularly seem to learn by watching a manipulator play them.

In general manipulators seem thoroughly to enjoy role playing. This is especially true if their manipulative bent is also characterized by a chameleon-like quality, that is, they can act as any member of the group on demand. Such a person can serve the group as an *ego crutch.* The person is instructed to be a helper to one or more members in a skit. The ego crutch can be directed to express a thought or feeling of a role-playing member who is fumbling or who is temporarily blocked in playing.

Level Three—Termination

Members who pass successfully through the five stages of the group will be those who have invested in it. They will have derived profit from it. They will view it with pleasure and warmth, as it has seved as an emotional haven. For these reasons communication activities for members in the termination stage can have sustained impact. Three are suggested here: the crystal ball, the wish bowl, and structuring for follow-up.

In the first of these, terminating members are handed an object that could pass for a *crystal ball* and asked to predict what they will be doing, how they will be functioning, six months hence. The ball is then passed to the other members and each asked to predict how the terminating members will be functioning six months hence. The purpose is to encourage graduating members by providing them with optimistic expectations and the memory of the group's support.

In the wish bowl activity, group members are asked to take a few moments silently to consider their *wishes* for the departing member, and then paper is distributed on which they write these down. The papers with the wishes are placed in a *bowl,* which can be presented to the terminating member as a gift from the group.

The group's influence can extend beyond actual membership if the leader structures for follow-up. Two ways are specifically recommended.

At their final meeting, for example, the terminating members can *write letters to themselves* describing how they feel at the moment and why they think they do. The leader then asks them to seal the letters and explains that they will be mailed to them on the date they specify on the envelope.

Or a terminating member is asked to set a *visiting date* on which he or she will return to share the group experience and/or describe post-group living with the group in session.

SUMMARY

THE CRITERIA for group activities should address two questions: What goal does the leader hope to attain? What member or group needs will be met? Other criteria should be concerned with leader expertise, appropriateness with regard to the age and interests of the group members, maximum sharing of profits by the members, the choice-retention rights of the members, and the learning derived from an applicability of the activity.

Listening activities include reiterating and reflecting, questioning and probing.

Communication activities can be understood to take place on three levels: (1) breaking the ice, (2) learning and maintaining, and (3) terminating.

Author Index

Subject Index

ABOUT THE AUTHOR

Joseph F. Perez, Ph.D., is Professor of Psychology at Westfield State College in Massachusetts. His courses include seminars in the dynamics of alcoholism and he directs workshops for in-service professionals on techniques for counseling the alcoholic. Dr. Perez is in private practice in Northampton, Mass. He has published extensively.